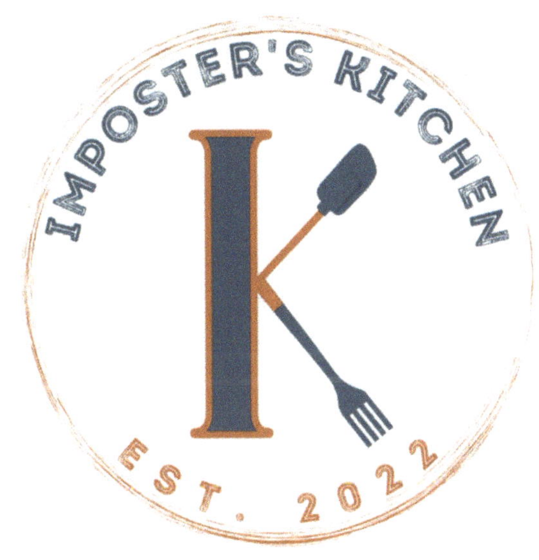

the

IMPOSTER'S KITCHEN

cookbook

By Abigail Martel

Disclaimer: some recipes inspired by or adapted from: half baked harvest, food network, my mom, my family, simply recipes, as well as restaurant menus and meals i've eaten and loved and recreated at home! thanks to all for their inspiration.

ISBN: 979-8-218-10537-2

Dedication

if you have ever asked me "what's for dinner?"
if you have answered my call when I wonder "does this sound good to you?"
if you have said "teach me how to cook like you can!"
if you've been at my kitchen table, sharing a meal with me,
if you believed in me when I didn't believe in myself.

this book is for you.

and for william, my sous chef (even though he cannot read and is a dog). always underfoot and ready to help with cleanup.

and jennie b, who inspired me to get it done, despite the self doubt... despite the *imposter* syndrome.

xoxo
abby

Introduction

my goal for this book was to create great recipes and fabulous food that is pretty, delicious, versatile, and most of all, approachable. in fact, many of these recipes came to be because i had a bunch of random basic ingredients on hand and no desire to go to the store and somehow made dinner happen with what i had. i cooked everything you see here, i took all the photos, and ate some really tasty food in the process.

the recipes are easily adapted for veggie diets if you use plant-based milk or butter, or use meat alternatives (or even omit it) where applicable. there is room for experimentation in almost every recipe, even for the most inexperienced cooks. you'll find boxes with text that include suggestions, tips, and my favorite cooking hacks to make your life and your kitchen experience a little easier. at the very least, i hope to show everyone that food is a universal love language, and when you get comfortable cooking stuff you like, it doesn't have to be something you dread at the end of the day.

i decided to title this book imposter's kitchen. if you're not familiar with the term 'imposter syndrome,' (also known as impostor syndrome, or impostor phenomenon) here is an explanation:

"...*impostor phenomenon occurs among high achievers who are unable to internalize and accept their success. They often attribute their accomplishments to luck rather than to ability, and fear that others will eventually unmask them as a fraud.*"[A.]

it's something i struggle with in many parts of my life. i wonder if I'll ever really 'make it.' if any of this is even worth trying for? is success in the food world even possible for a home cook with a boring desk job like me? what gives me the competetive edge over anyone else to break into an industry that takes years of grueling, greasy kitchen work, late nights, and formal culinary education? the fact of the matter is that I won't ever know unless i give it my best shot. so here it is.

every book purchased is a little step closer to accomplishing my goals. i cannot express how much I appreciate your support. i hope to serve you in my future restaurant some day.

most of all, i hope you enjoy this book and all of the wonderful things you'll create with it. reach out on instagram sometime to chat food, ask questions, and follow along on my culinary journey.

PS- excuse the probably incorrect footnote format, it's been a while since english class. i did my best.

A. Weir, Kirsten, 'Feel Like a Fraud?', *American Psychological Association,* https://www.apa.org/gradpsych/2013/11/fraud

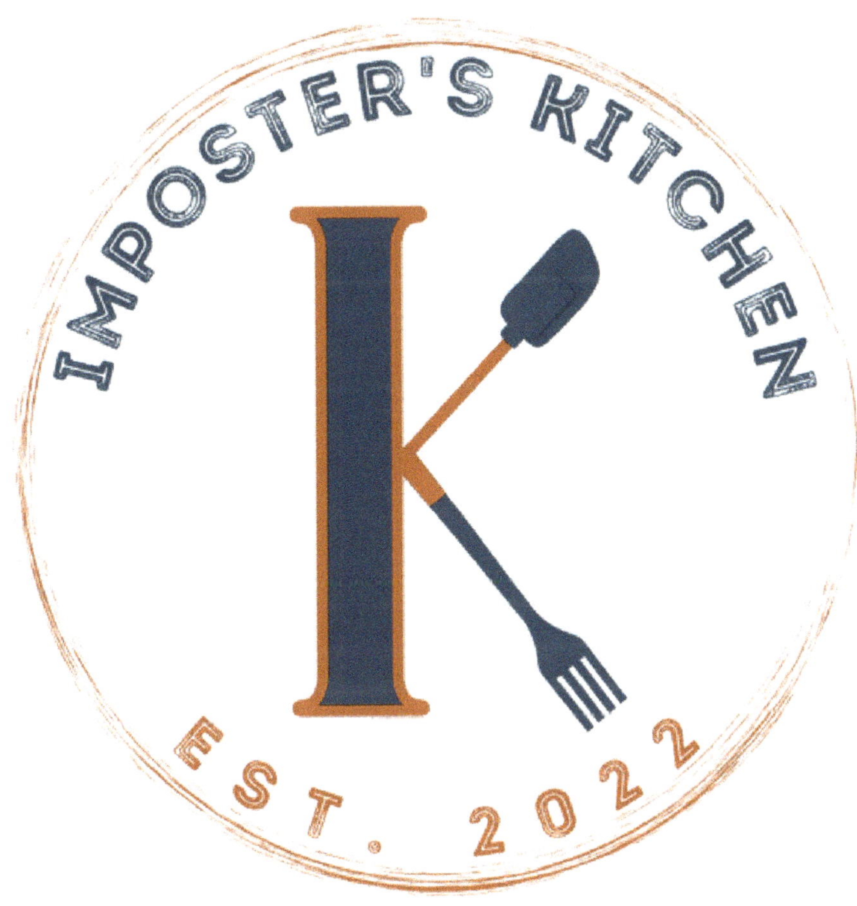
IMPOSTER'S KITCHEN
K
EST. 2022

CONTENTS

APPS, SIDES + SNACKS

BRUNCH + BREADS

HANDHELDS

SALADS

SOUPS + STEWS

MEATS + MARINADES

SWEETS

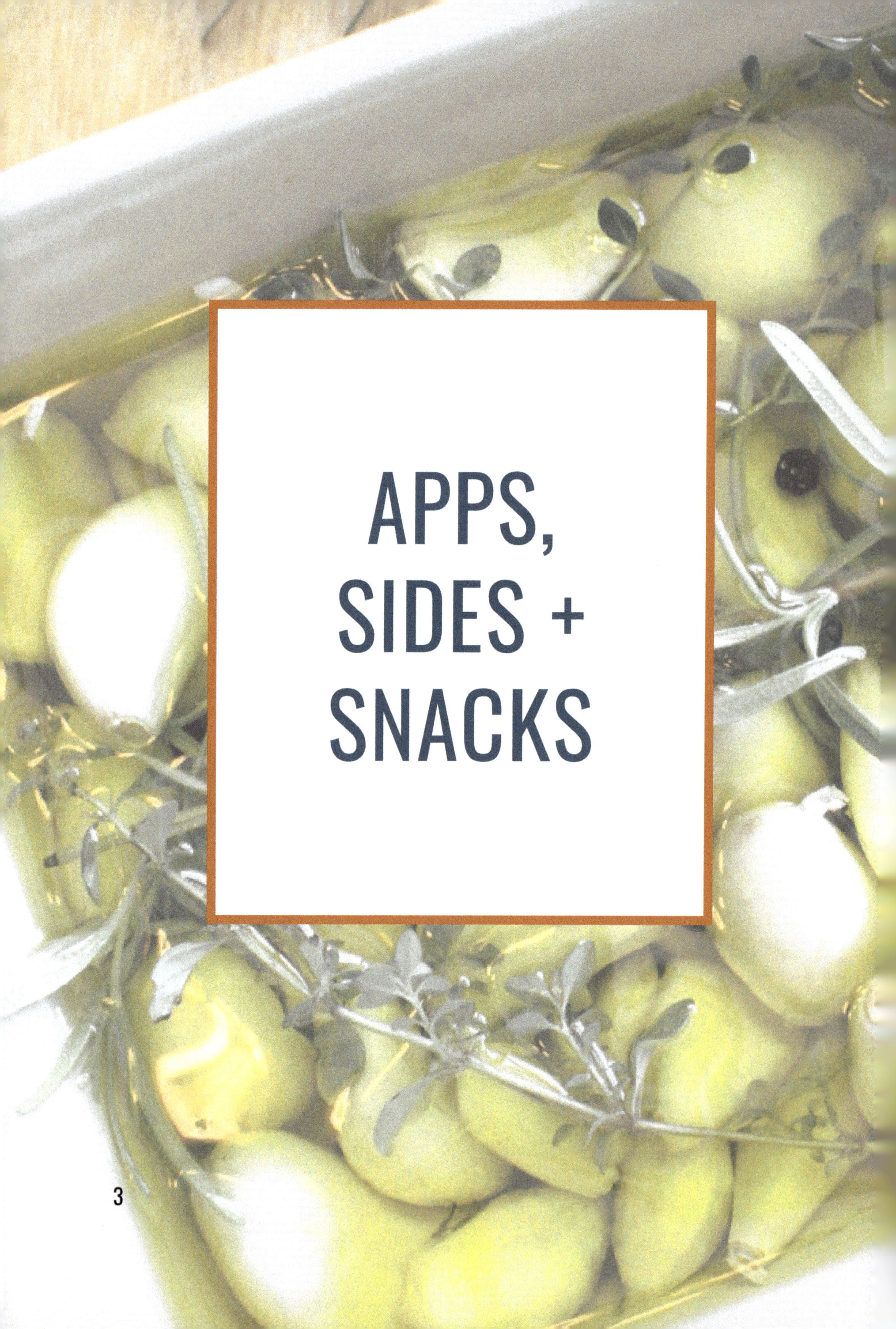

APPS, SIDES + SNACKS

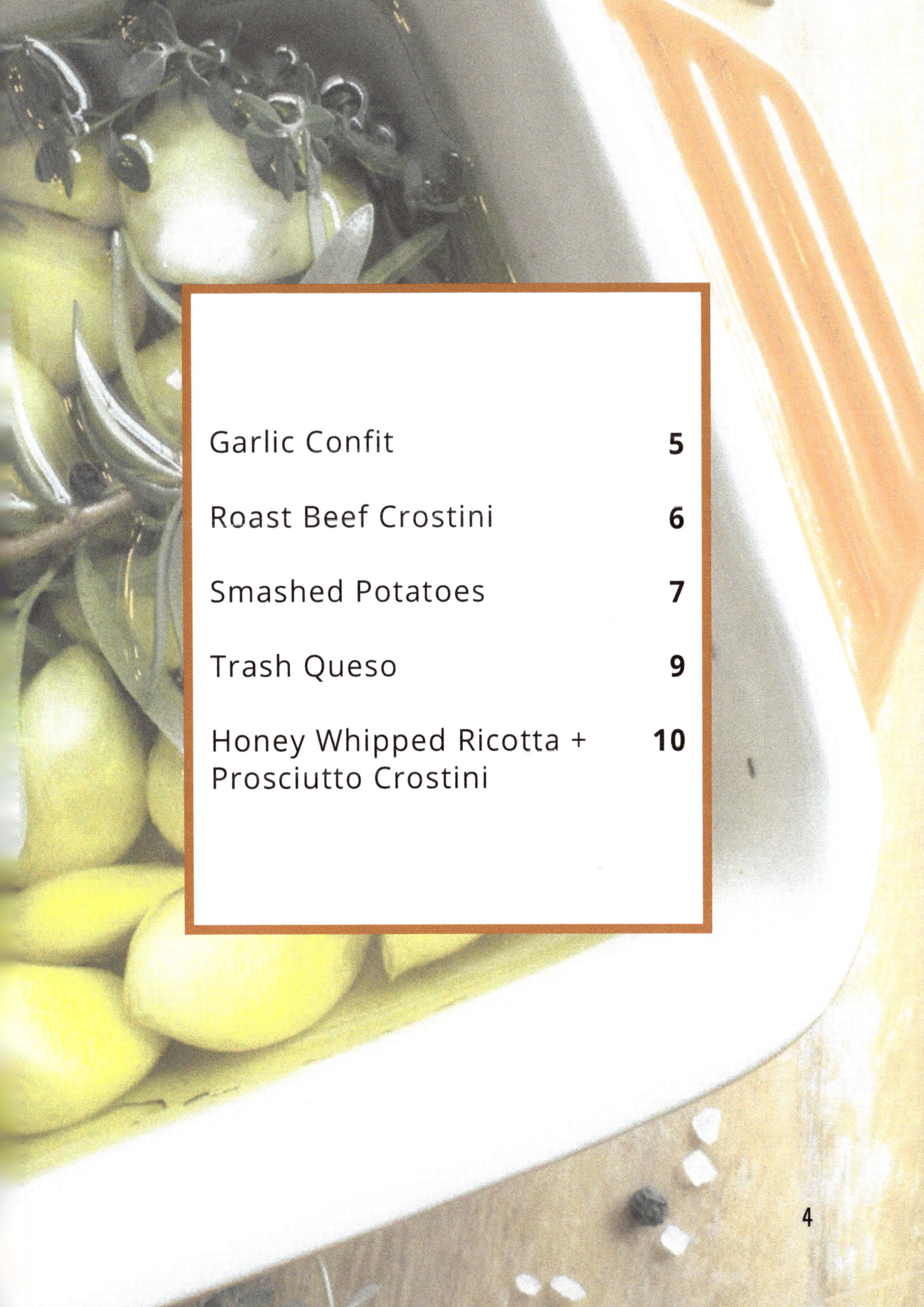

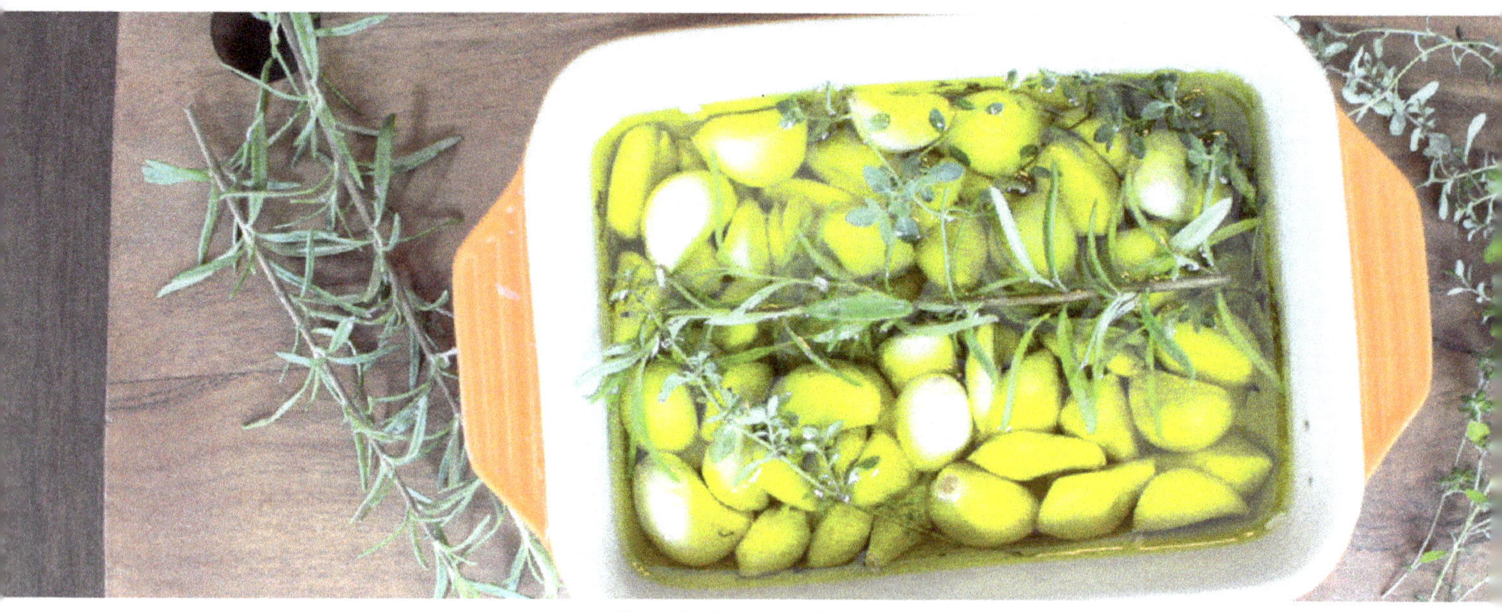

GARLIC CONFIT

YIELD: 1 1/2 CUPS PREP TIME: 10 MIN COOKING TIME: 2 HOURS

An easy recipe with two delicious results: rich, spreadable garlic cloves and a deeply flavor-infused garlic oil. The possibilities are endless when it comes to garlic. It is important to note that this needs to be stored properly in the refrigerator or freezer and never at room temperature. Experiment with flavor and add your favorite herbs to the oil before cooking.

Ingredients

- 3 large bulbs of garlic, cloves peeled
- 1 1/2 c olive oil or grapeseed oil
- fresh herbs if desired (thyme, basil, rosemary, oregano)

Directions

1. Preheat oven to 250 F.
2. Place whole, peeled garlic cloves in a small oven-safe dish or pan, and cover with oil. Use a smaller pan or more oil if cloves are not fully submerged.
3. Cover and bake in 250 degree oven for 2 hours or until the cloves are lightly browned and tender. Your house is going to smell amazing.
4. Once the oil has cooled off, transfer the garlic and oil to an airtight container or jar to store in the refrigerator for up to one week, or in the freezer for up to three months.

i highly recommend starting with this recipe. having the infused oil as well as the tender roasted garlic on hand to use in many recipes lets you skip a step.

ROAST BEEF CROSTINI
WITH HORSERADISH AIOLI

YIELD: 12 SERVINGS   PREP TIME: 10 MIN   COOKING TIME: 10 MIN

Savory roast beef with caramelized onions and a tangy horseradish aioli... A simple and elegant starter. Make this in a snap by using rare roast beef from the deli counter or take the long(ish) way and roast your own.

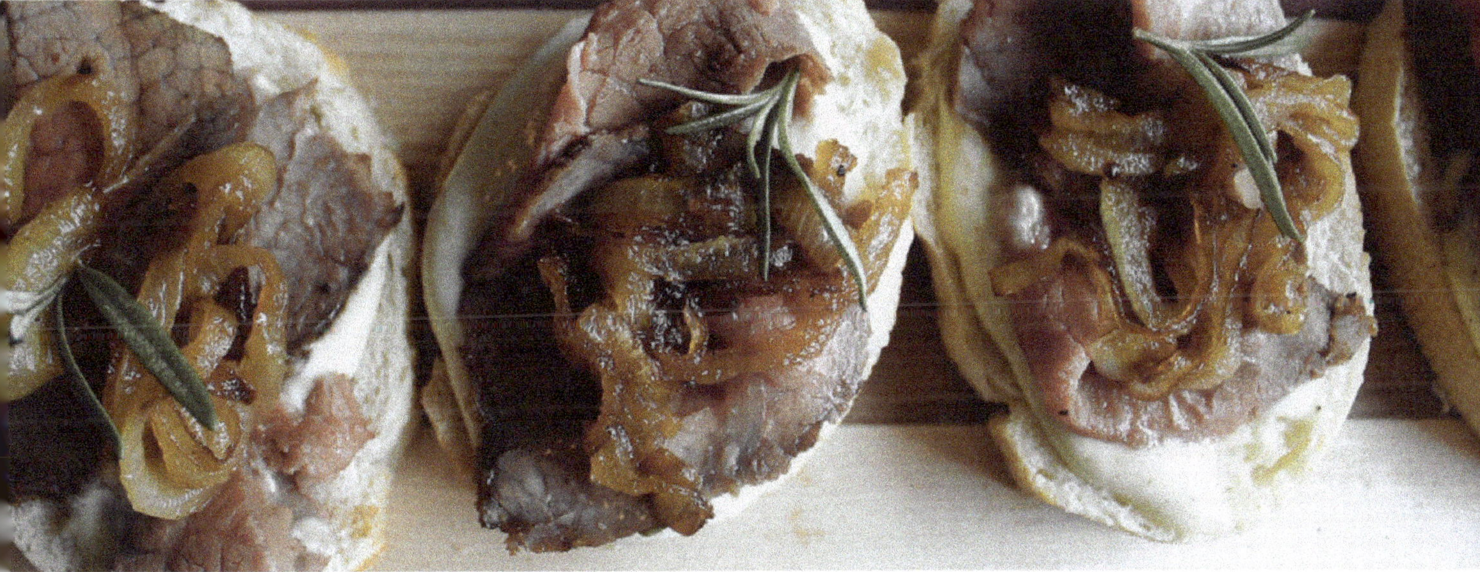

Ingredients

- 1 french baguette
- 1 tbs olive oil plus more for brushing
- 1 thinly sliced yellow onion
- 2 tbs butter
- 1/2 lb rare roast beef
- 1/4 c mayonnaise
- 1 tbs minced garlic
- 2 tbs horseradish
- 1 tbs lemon juice
- salt + pepper to taste

Directions

1. Preheat oven to 350 F. Slice the baguette into 1/2 inch thick pieces and place in a single layer on a baking sheet. Brush lightly with olive oil + season with salt and pepper.
2. Lightly toast both sides of the bread in the oven, about 6 minutes each side, or until preferred toastiness level.
3. Halve the onion from root to tip and thinly slice the whole thing into half-moons. Saute in a pan with butter on medium-low heat until browned, fragrant and caramelized, about 10 minutes.
4. Mix together the mayonnaise, garlic, lemon juice, horseradish til well combined to make the aioli. Add more seasonings to taste.
5. Spread the aioli on each slice of toasted bread. Top with a folded piece of roast beef and garnish with caramelized onions.
6. Finish with salt and pepper and serve immediately.

SMASHED POTATOES

YIELD: 6-8 SERVINGS PREP TIME: 30 MIN COOKING TIME: 30-40 MIN

Potato people, this is for you. Can you imagine the love child of twice baked potatoes + potatoes au gratin? This is pretty much it, but much less labor-intensive. No pun intended.

Ingredients

- 1 lb creamer potatoes
- 4 tbs butter
- salt + pepper
- 2 cloves garlic, minced
- 1 tbs basil
- 1 tbs parsley
- 1/4 c grated parmesan cheese plus more for garnish
- 1/2 c shredded mozzarella, divided in 2 equal portions

Directions

1. Drop the potatoes, skin-on, into a pot of heavily salted boiling water, over high heat, for 30 minutes or until soft.
2. While the potatoes are cooking, preheat your oven to 400 F.
3. Melt the butter in a small bowl and mix in the seasonings, parmesan cheese, and garlic. Spread evenly on the bottom of a 9x13 pan and sprinkle half of the mozzarella on top of the butter mixture.
4. Drain the water from the potatoes, let them cool until you can safely handle them.
5. Cut each potato in half. Place the potatoes cut-side down in rows on top of the butter and cheese in the pan. Put in as many as you can fit!
6. Using the bottom of a drinking glass or other flat-bottomed implement, gently squish each potato into a flat shape, and top with the other half of the mozzarella.
7. Bake uncovered for 30-40 minutes or until crispy, golden brown. Top with a dusting of parmesan and serve as an app or a side dish!

use a splash of the infused oil from the garlic confit recipe in addition to the butter to ramp up the flavor. serve these with bacon bits, a drizzle of sour cream + sliced chives for a potato-skins style dish!

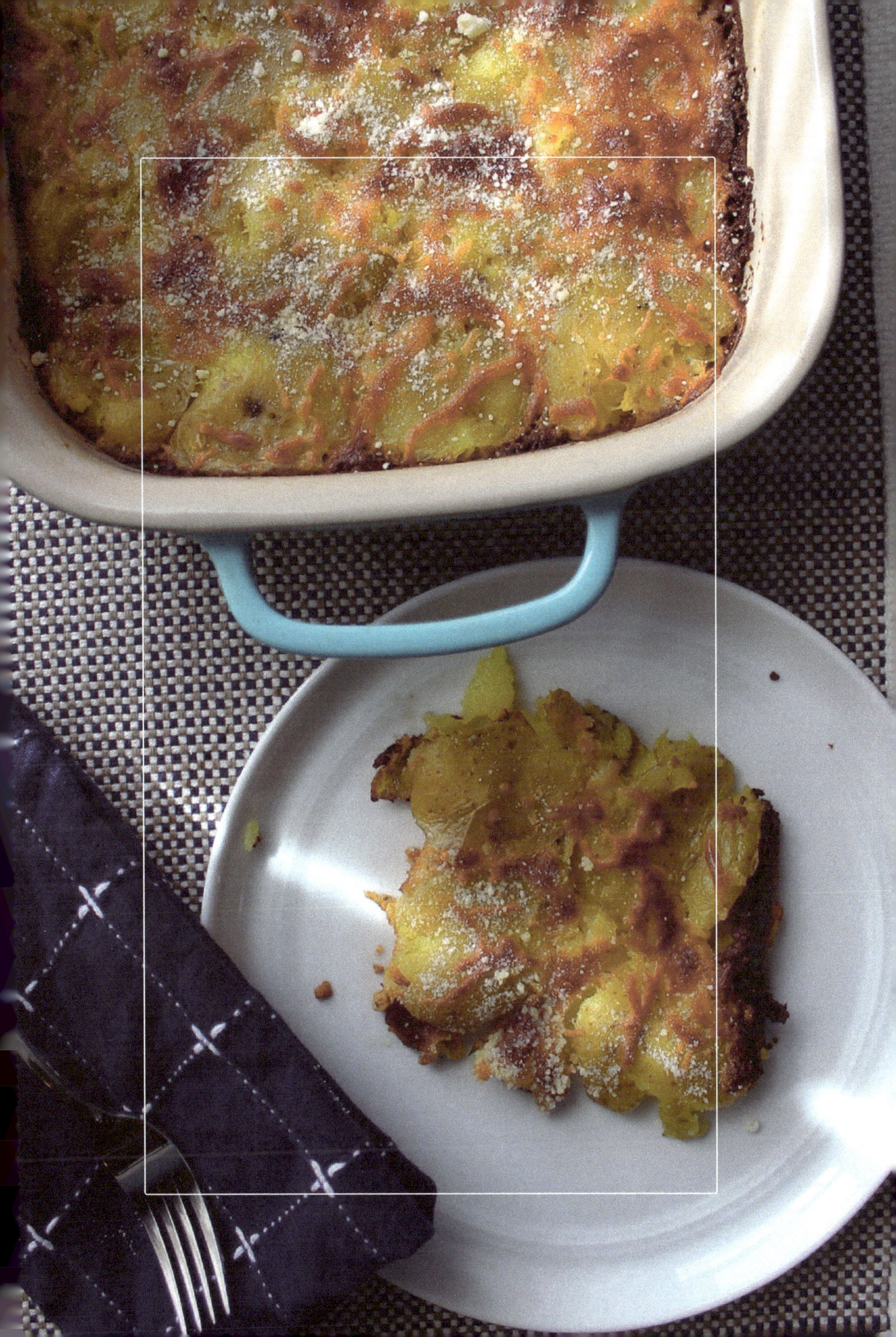

TRASH QUESO

YIELD: PARTY SIZE PREP TIME: 10 MIN COOKING TIME: 30 MIN

This queso dip is a hit at every party. We've put it on top of tacos, burgers and hot dogs, in quesadillas, and of course it's delicious with tortilla chips too. Quick crockpot prep + plug makes it easy for even the busiest person to whip up.

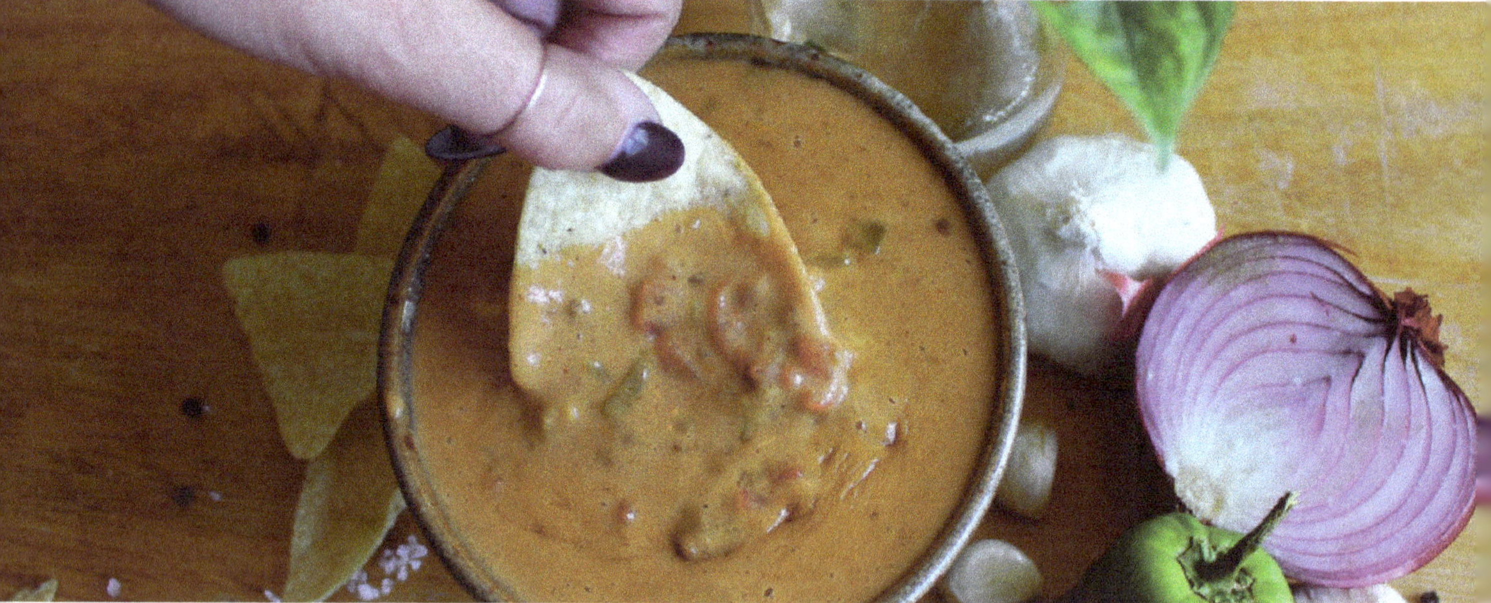

Ingredients

- 1 lb block of original Velveeta cheese
- 10 oz can of diced tomatoes and green chilies, drained
- 4 oz can diced green chilies or jalapenos, drained
- 15 oz can of Hormel Chili (any variety- we prefer chili no beans)

Directions

1. Insert crock pot liner (if using) into a 4+ quart crock pot. The recipe will have to be split if using a smaller crock pot.
2. Add in all ingredients: cheese, tomatoes, chilies, and chili. At this point, throw in any extras desired as well.
3. Turn crock pot to low and cover for 20-30 minutes, or until melted.
4. Mix to incorporate all ingredients.
5. Turn the crock pot to the keep warm setting. Serve with tortilla chips and watch it disappear.

---

queso is easy to make to suit your taste. it is pretty mild as-is, but try adding fresh diced jalapenos, poblanos, chilies, or classic Mexican spices like cumin , cayenne, or chili powder to make it more spicy.

HONEY WHIPPED RICOTTA + PROSCIUTTO CROSTINI

YIELD: 10-12 SERVINGS PREP TIME: 15 MIN ASSEMBLY TIME: 10 MIN

In this recipe, the lightly sweetened and mild ricotta perfectly pairs with classic prosciutto. The whipped ricotta can be made up to two days in advance. Brighten the flavor of these bites up with a piece of cantaloupe or grilled peach in addition to the prosciutto.

Ingredients

- 2 c whole milk ricotta
- 2 tbs heavy cream
- 3 tbs honey + more for garnish
- 1 tsp thyme
- salt and pepper to taste
- 6 oz thin sliced prosciutto
- 1 baguette cut into 1" slices and toasted or grilled

Directions

1. In a blender, food processor, or with a hand mixer, combine ricotta, honey, thyme and cream on high speed until silky smooth. Season to taste with salt and pepper.
2. To assemble ahead of time, spread the whipped ricotta atop each crostini, and top with a piece of prosciutto. Lightly drizzle with honey and serve immediately.
3. For a more DIY and travel-friendly approach, serve the ricotta in a bowl and arrange the prosciutto and crostini on a board or plate for guests to build their own.

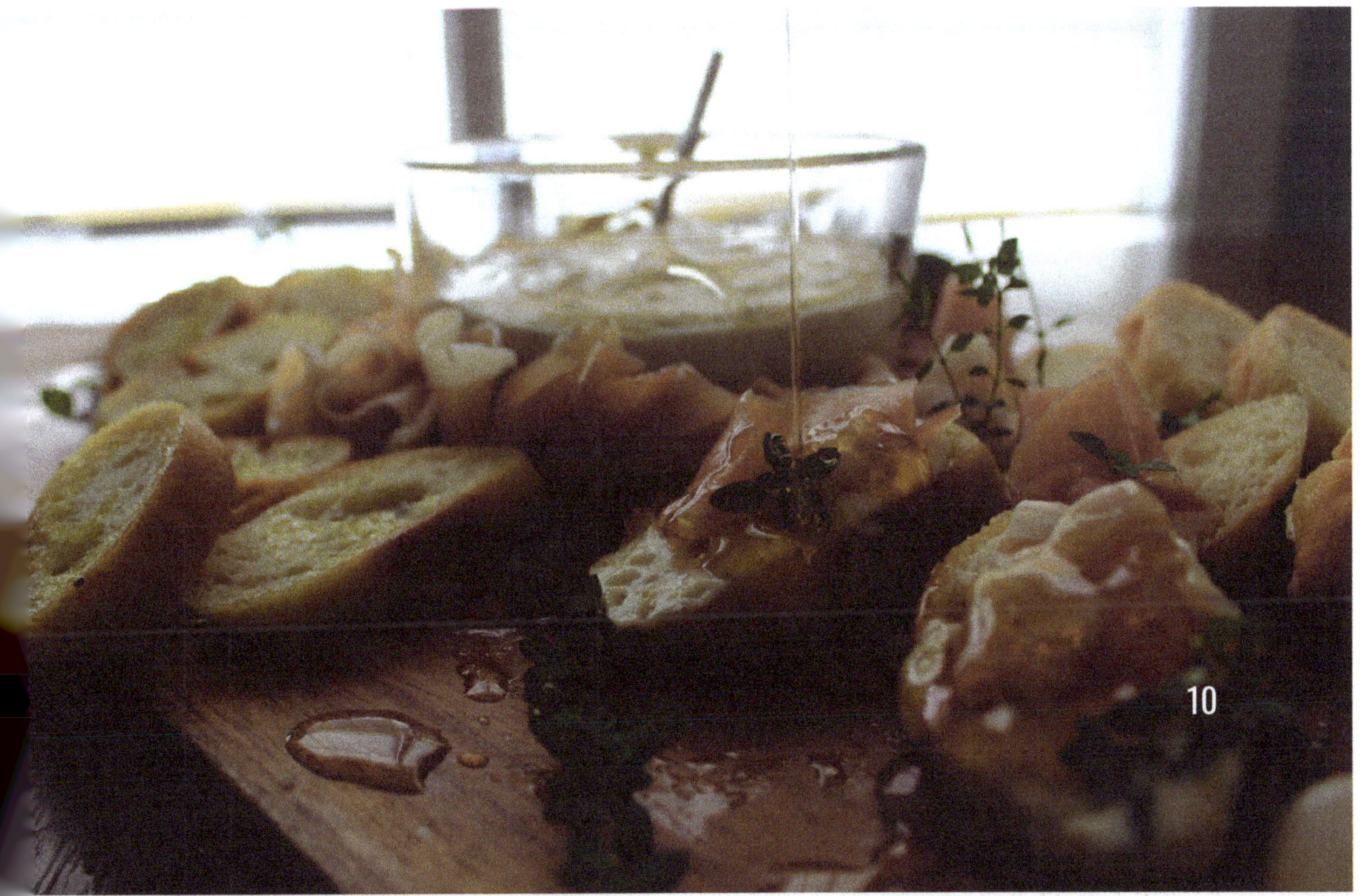

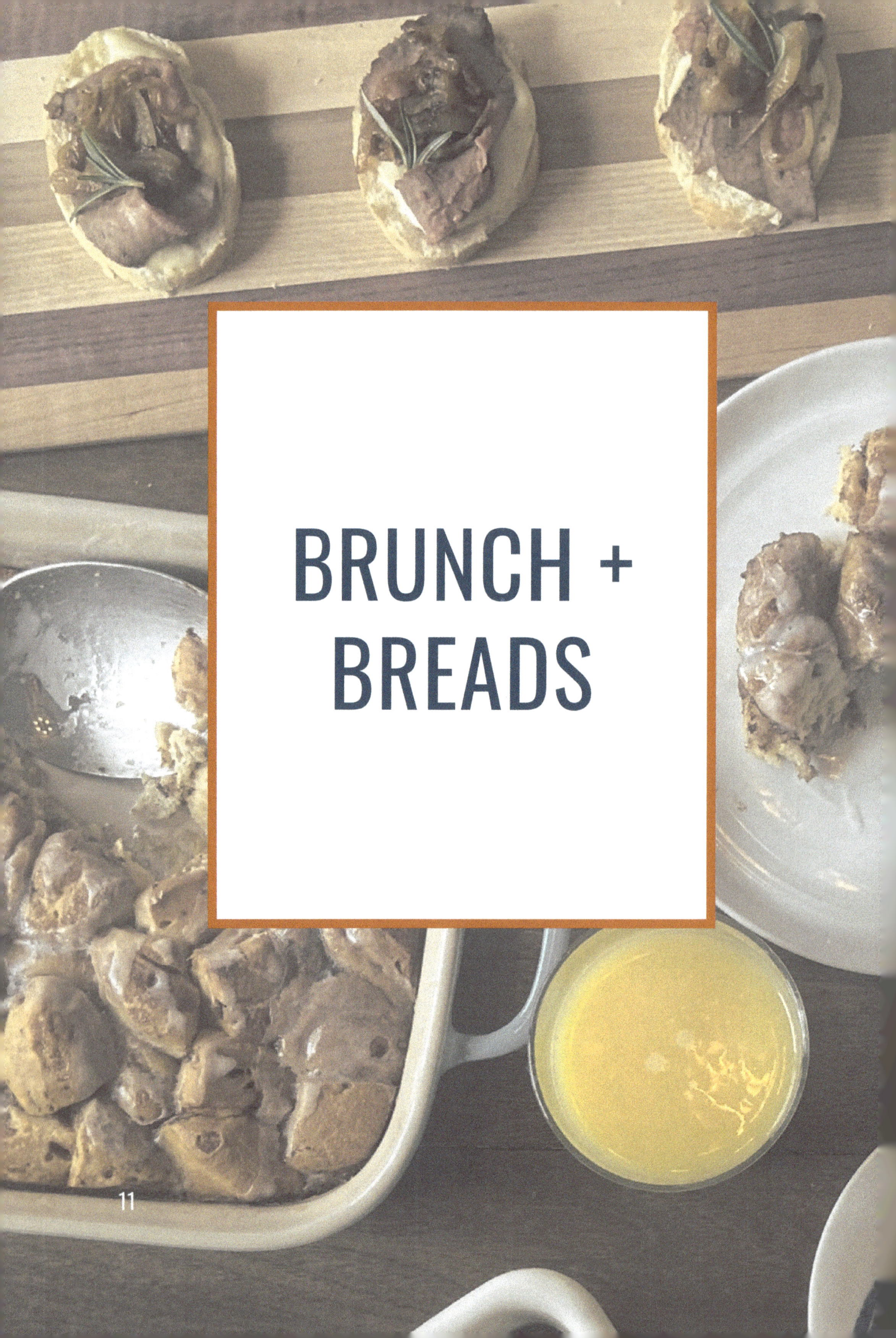

BRUNCH + BREADS

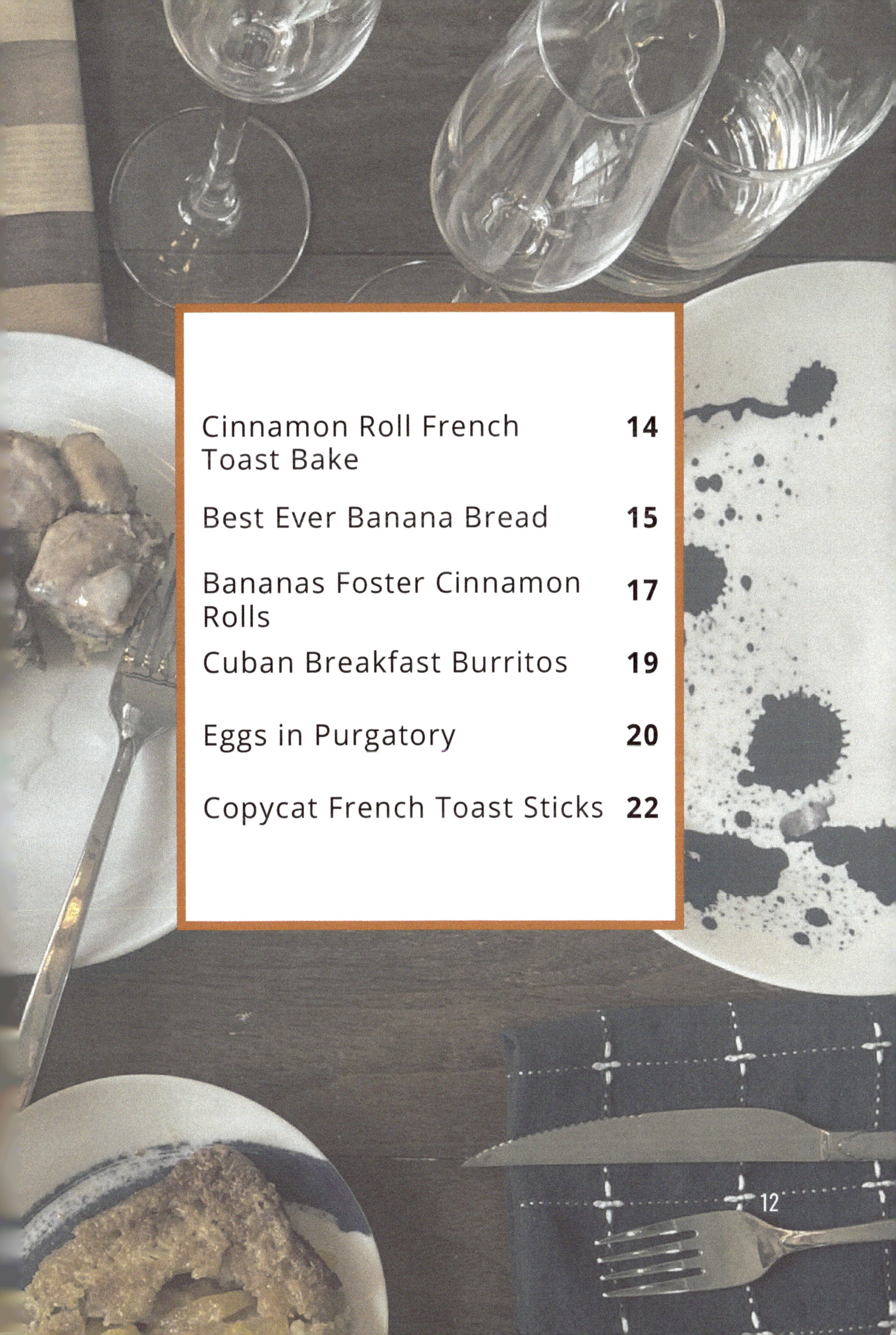

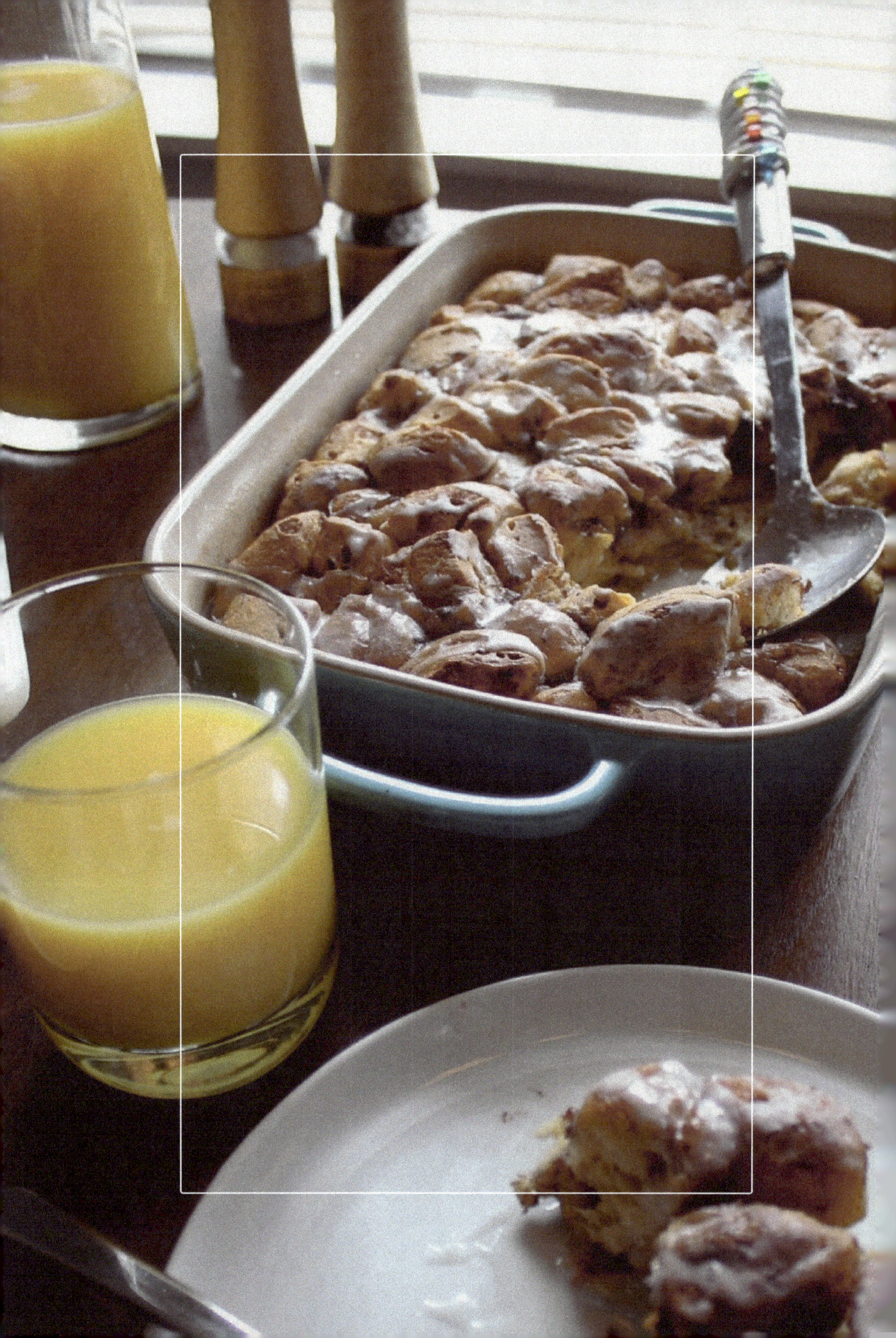

CINNAMON ROLL FRENCH TOAST BAKE

YIELD: 6-8 SERVINGS   PREP TIME: 10 MIN/OVERNIGHT   COOKING TIME: 25 MIN

Great for holiday mornings with friends or family. This recipe feeds a crowd, and can be made the night before serving, to minimize morning mess and kitchen chaos; in fact, it's even better if you let it sit overnight.

Ingredients

- 2 tubes of refrigerated cinnamon rolls, quartered (raw)
- 4 tbs melted butter
- 3 eggs, beaten
- 1/4 c milk
- 1 tsp ground cinnamon
- 1 tsp ground nutmeg
- 1/2 tsp vanilla extract
- 1/2 c maple syrup

Directions

1. Cut each raw cinnamon roll into quarters.
2. In a large bowl, whisk together the eggs, milk, cinnamon, nutmeg, and vanilla.
3. Pour melted butter in the bottom of a 9x13 casserole dish, and spread the quartered cinnamon rolls evenly over the butter.
4. Pour the egg mixture over the cinnamon roll pieces, and drizzle the maple syrup over the top. Let it sit for 10 minutes while the oven pre heats prior to baking- but is even better if you wait overnight. This bake can be made up to a day in advance!
5. Bake at 375 F for 25-30 minutes or until the top is golden brown.
6. Serve with a drizzle of icing from the cinnamon roll packaging and or maple syrup!

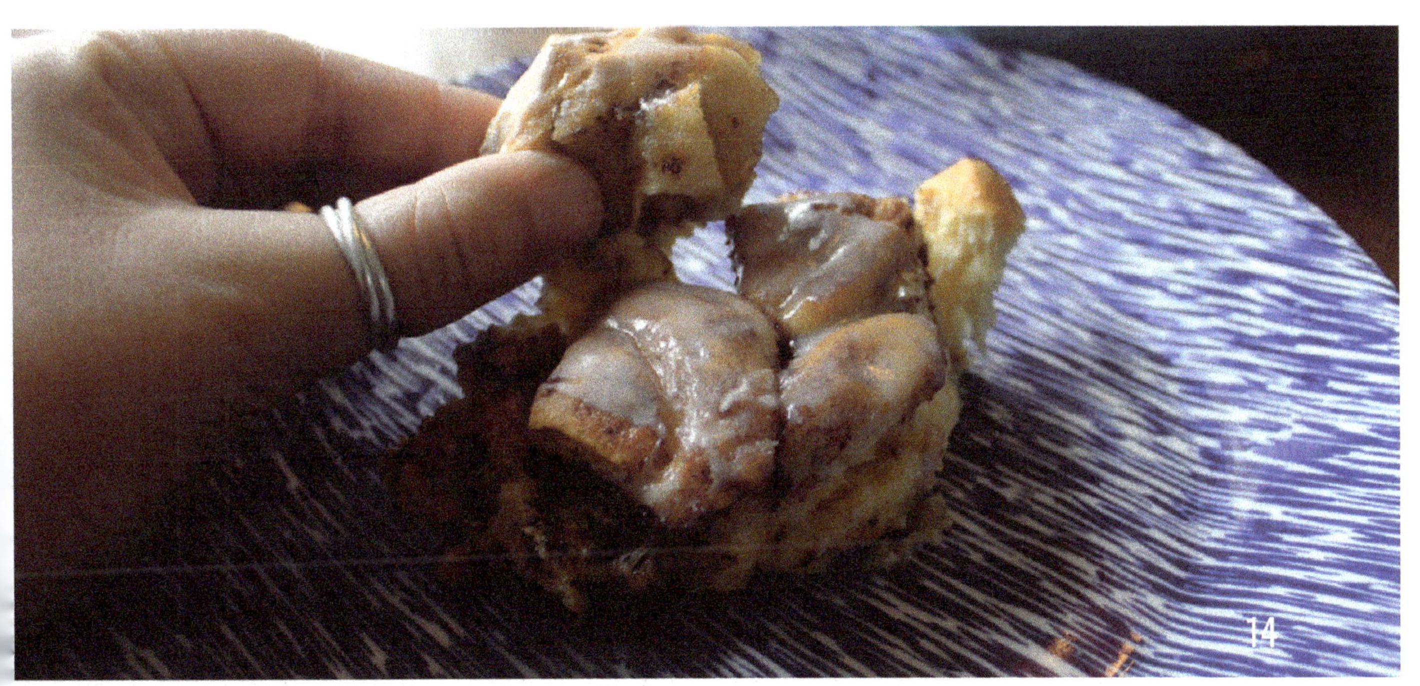

BEST EVER BANANA BREAD

YIELD: 1 LOAF PREP TIME: 8 MIN COOKING TIME: 1 HOUR

This is a recipe EVERYONE will ask you for. Enough said.

Ingredients

- 3-4 over-ripened bananas, thawed if previously frozen
- 1/3 c melted butter
- 1 egg
- 3/4 c sugar
- 1 tsp vanilla
- 2 tbs sour cream
- 1 tsp baking soda
- pinch of salt
- 1 1/2 c flour

Directions

1. Preheat oven to 350 F. Grease a 4x8 loaf pan and set aside.
2. In a large bowl, mash bananas using a fork.
3. Mix in the melted butter to the mashed bananas. Once incoporated, mix in the egg, sugar, sour cream, and vanilla.
4. Sprinkle the salt and baking soda over the mixture and stir briefly.
5. Once combined, mix in the flour and fold in any mix-ins desired.
6. Immediately pour the batter into the greased loaf pan and bake for one hour or until a knife stuck into the center comes out clean.
7. Cool completely before cutting and serve.

sour cream can be substituted by yogurt or apple sauce, or omitted entirely, but trust me on this- it makes this banana bread dense, hearty, and moist. (i'm so sorry for using the M-word)

aside from nuts or chocolate chips, other tasty mix-ins include coconut flakes, blueberries, butterscotch chips, a dash of cinnamon, or using almond extract instead of vanilla.

if you opt to bake this in a more shallow pan or lined muffin tins, check the doneness around 30 minutes.

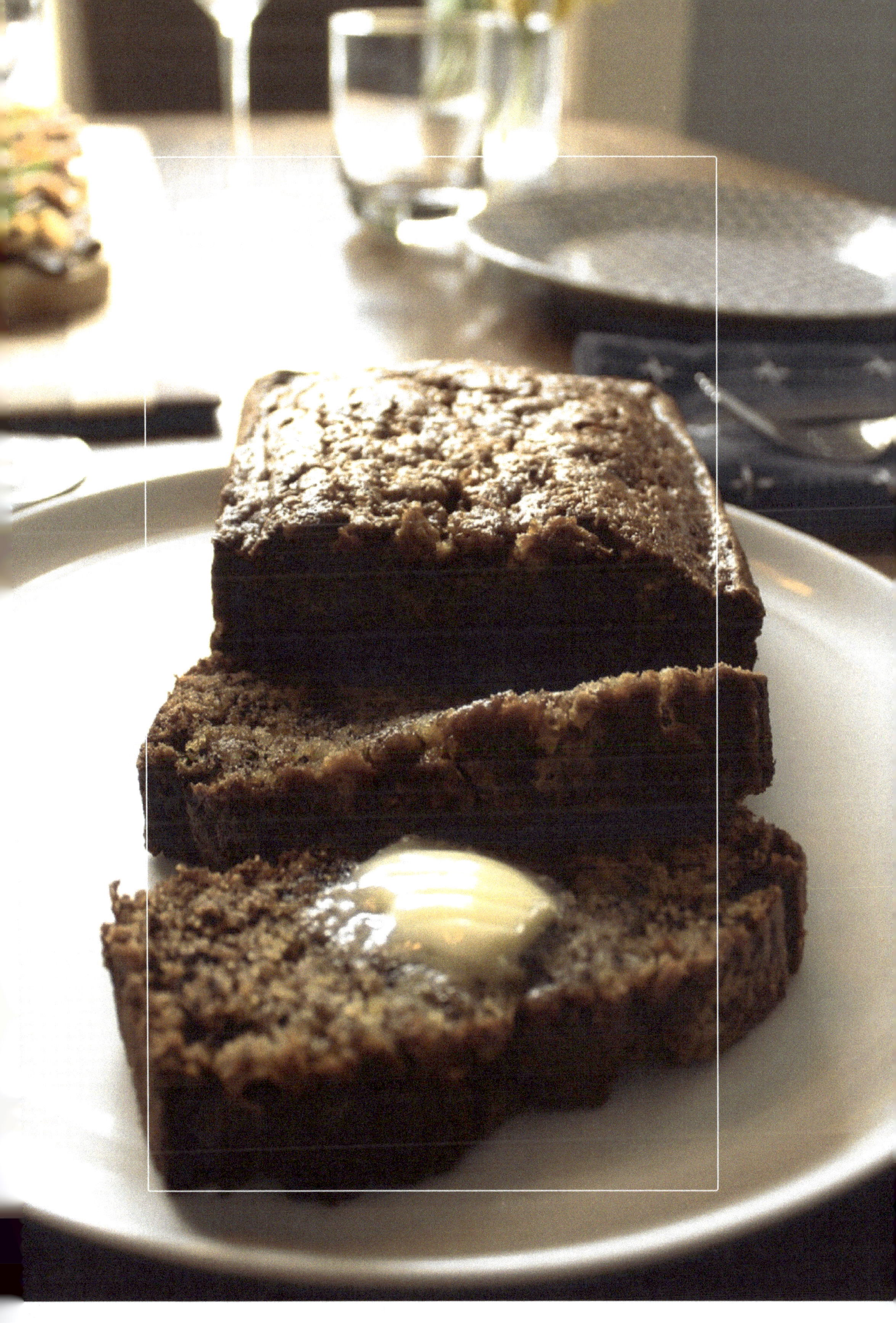

BANANAS FOSTER CINNAMON ROLLS

YIELD: 6-8 ROLLS PREP TIME: 1.25 HOURS COOKING TIME: 25 MIN

Waiting for the dough to rise is like, 70% of the battle. These can easily be made vegan!

Ingredients

Dough

- 3 tbs butter
- 1 packet rapid-rise yeast
- 1 c milk
- 2 medium sized bananas
- 1 tbs sugar
- 1/4 tsp salt
- 3 1/2 c flour

Filling

- 3 tbs butter, melted
- 1 tbs bourbon , whiskey or rum flavored extract
- 1/3 c brown sugar
- 1 tbs cinnamon
- 1/2 tsp vanilla
- 1 mashed banana

Directions

1. In a large bowl, mash 2 medium bananas, mix in 1 cup of milk, and microwave for 1 minute or until hot, but not boiling. Once hot, melt the butter into the mixture.
2. Sprinkle the yeast over the banana, milk and butter mixture and let proof for 10 minutes or until foamy looking. If it doesn't get foamy, the yeast might be dead- if so, repeat steps 1 and 2 again with new yeast.
3. Once proofed, add in the sugar and salt and stir.
4. Add in the flour, 1/2 cup at a time, mixing as you go. You might not use all of the flour. Once dough becomes too sticky to stir, transfer to a floured surface and knead by hand for a minute until it forms a sticky, loose ball.
5. Rinse out and dry the mixing bowl, coat with oil and place the dough back in the bowl. Leave the dough in the bowl, covered, in a warm spot for 1 hour or until doubled in size.
6. While the dough is rising, make the filling. Mash one banana with the the bourbon (or rum extract), vanilla extract, brown sugar and cinnamon to make a paste. It should be on the dry side, so add more sugar if needed.
7. After allowing the dough to rise, place the dough on a floured surface and roll out into a 1/4 inch thick rectangle. Brush the dough with the melted butter, and spread the brown sugar filling on top. From the long edge closest to you, tightly roll the dough up into a log.
8. Once rolled, place the log seam-side down. Use a very sharp knife to cut into 2 inch sections. Wrap the cut sections tightly and freeze now if you plan to bake these at a later date.
9. Place dough sections cut side-up in a buttered, shallow baking dish. Brush the tops with melted butter or sprinke with additional brown sugar and nuts if desired, and let rise again while the oven preheats to 350 F.
10. Once preheated, bake for 25-35 minutes or until golden brown. Cool slightly before serving. We enjoy these with whipped cream!

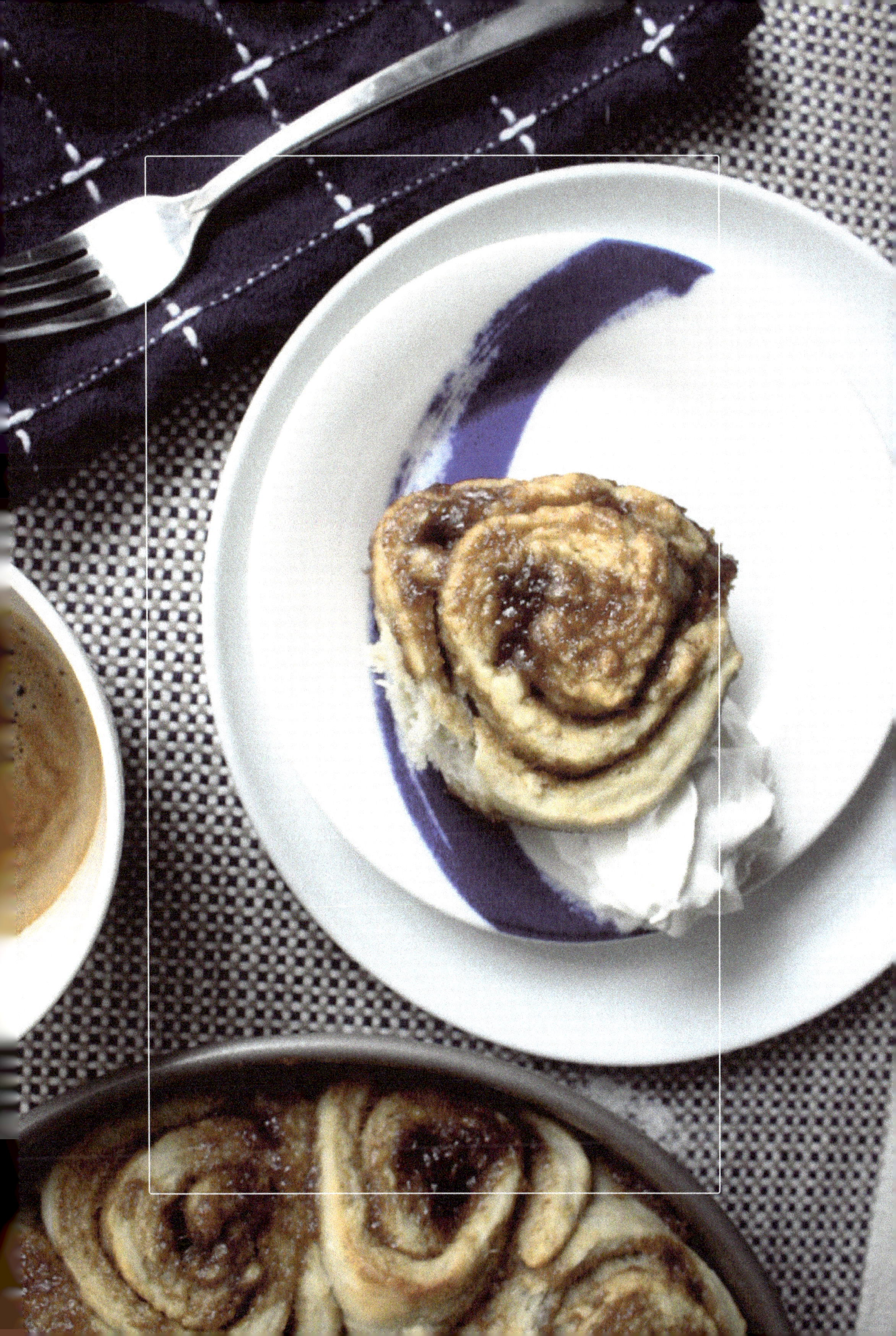

CUBAN BREAKFAST BURRITOS

YIELD: 2 BURRITOS PREP TIME: 5 MIN COOKING TIME: 5 MIN

For the kinds of people who might have a tendency to skip straight to dinner leftovers for breakfast... I present to you: the best of both worlds. Use store bought pulled pork or leftovers of the homemade goodness.

Ingredients

- 2 burrito size tortillas
- 2 slices of swiss cheese
- 4 eggs
- 1 tbs milk
- salt + pepper
- 1 tbs butter
- 1/2 c pulled pork
- 4 slices of black forest ham
- spicy mustard
- 1/4 c chopped sour pickles or dill relish

Directions

1. Prepare tortillas: spread mustard to taste over one side of each tortilla and place one slice of swiss cheese on top.
2. Melt butter in a nonstick pan over medium heat. Whisk eggs and milk together in a bowl and pour into the hot pan. Season to taste with salt and pepper, and scramble.
3. Place half of the scrambled eggs atop the swiss cheese on each tortilla.
4. Place the pan back on the burner, and warm up the ham and pulled pork until heated through (or use the microwave).
5. Once heated, place 2 pieces of ham and 1/4 c of the pulled pork on to each tortilla.
6. Roll the burritos, toast in the pan if desired (use a little piece of cheese at the seam as 'glue'), and serve immediately.

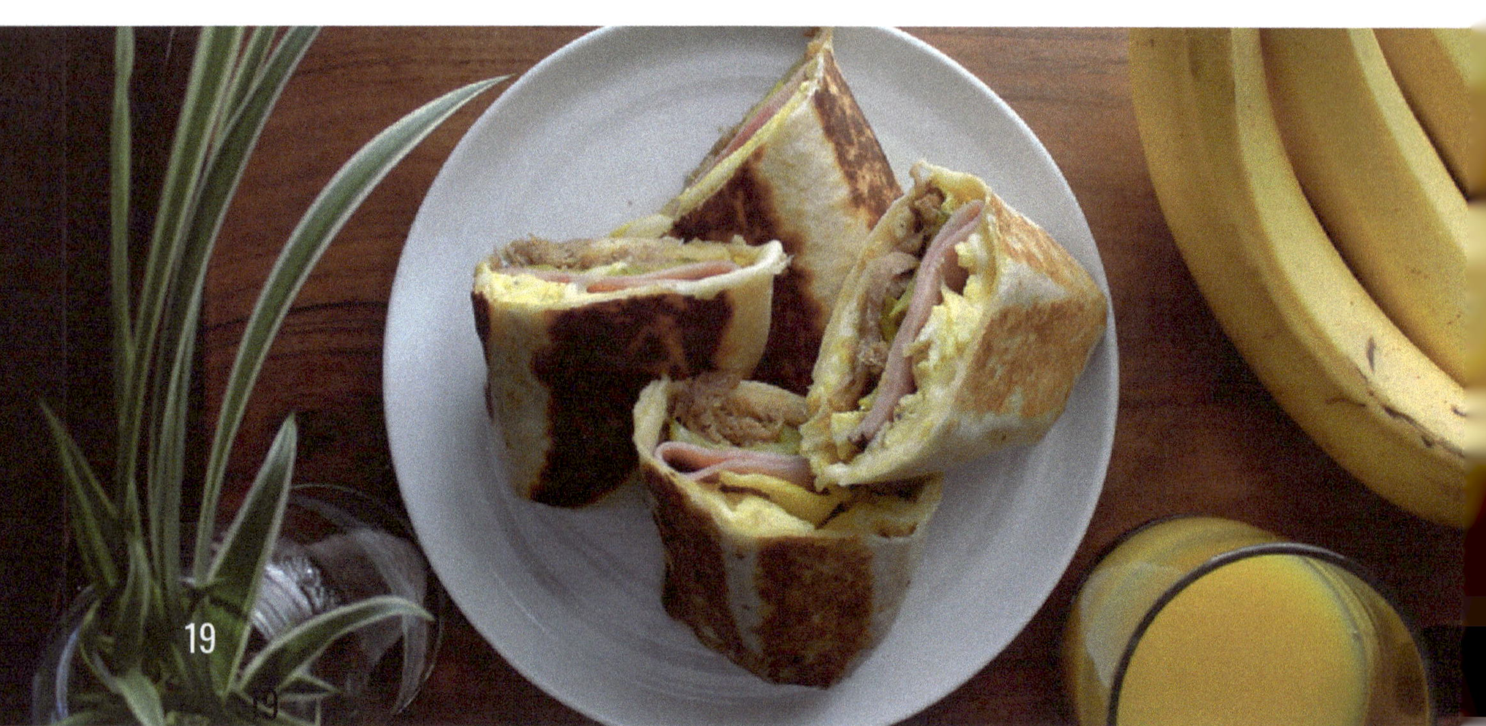

EGGS IN PURGATORY

YIELD: 3+ SERVINGS PREP TIME: 10 MIN COOKING TIME: 35 MIN

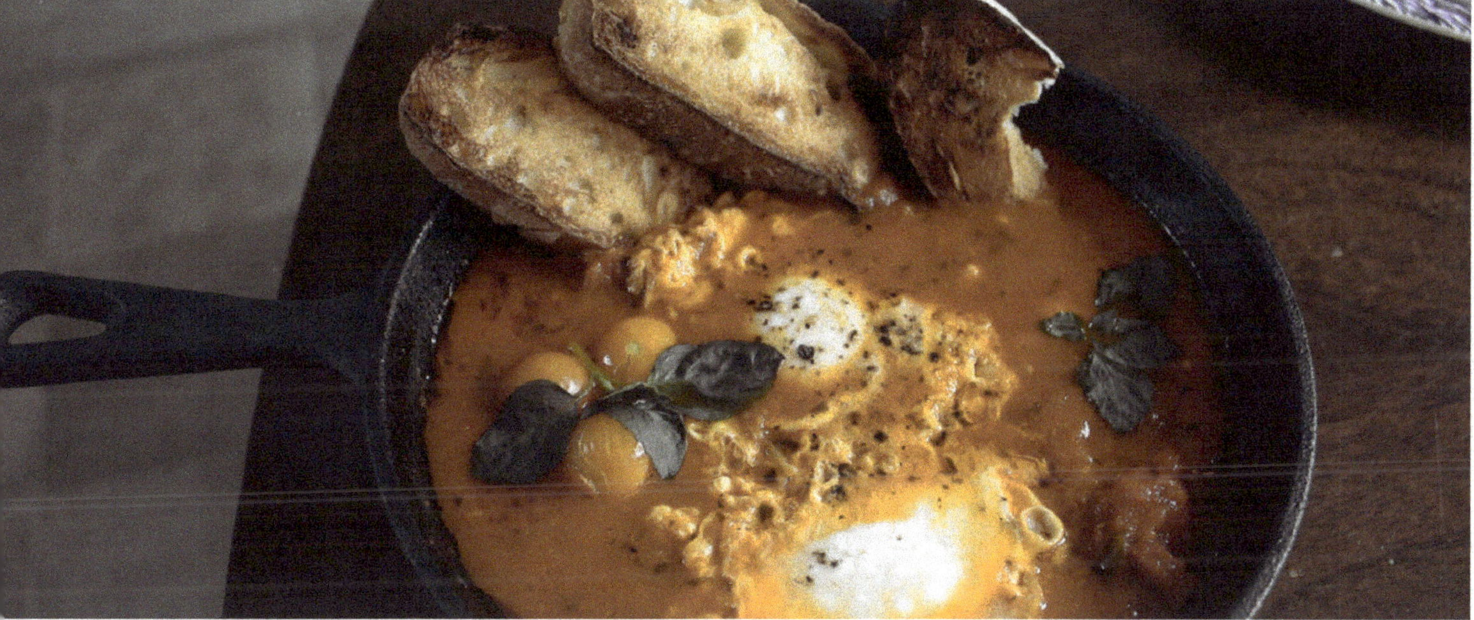

Ingredients

- 1 16 oz jar of tomato sauce or crushed tomatoes, any variety
- 6 eggs
- 1 finely chopped sweet onion
- 1 finely chopped bell pepper
- 3 tbs minced garlic
- cayenne, paprika cumin, salt, pepper, turmeric to taste
- (optional) in-season veggies like zucchini, spinach, kale, carrots, hot peppers, etc.
- grilled or toasted crusty bread like ciabatta or sourdough

Directions

1. Chop the onion and pepper and mince the garlic.
2. Heat 2 tbs oil or butter in a large, shallow pan. Cook pepper, onion and garlic together until fragrant.
3. Add tomato sauce to the pan as well as any in-season veggies you like, and season to taste with cayenne, paprika, cumin, turmeric, salt, and pepper. The liquid in the pan should be a little over an inch deep, add a bit of water if needed. Let simmer for 10-15 minutes, stirring occasionally.
4. After 10-15 minutes and while the sauce is steadily simmering, create divots in the mixture with the back of a spoon or ladle, and gently crack one egg into each divot.
5. Cover the pan and let simmer over low heat until the egg whites are cooked and the yolk is slightly soft, about 8-10 minutes.
6. Serve eggs with a scoop of sauce. Top with feta, shredded cheese and any herbs you like, and serve with a hearty, crusty bread to soak up all the sauce.

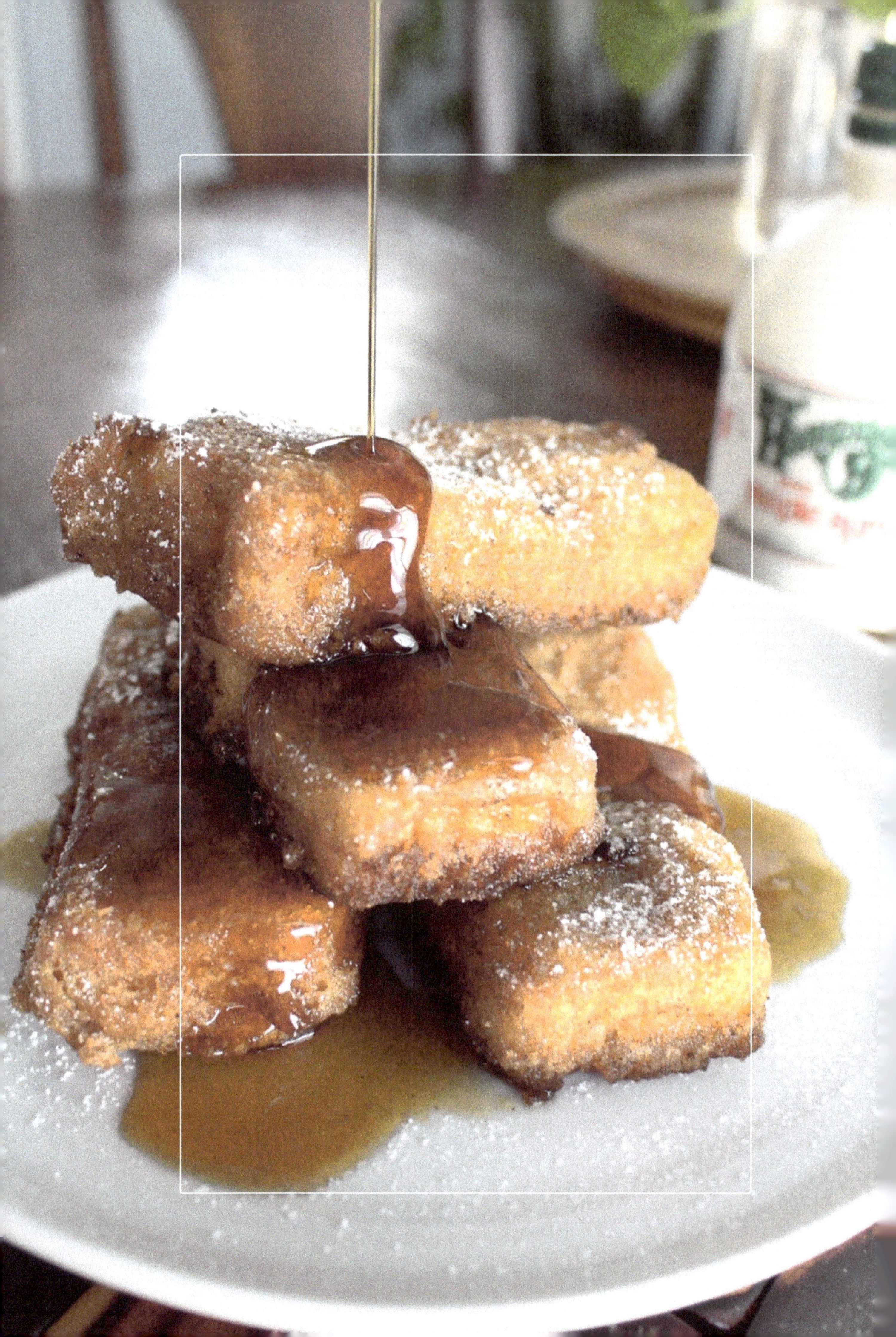

COPYCAT FRENCH TOAST STICKS

YIELD: 12 STICKS/4 SERVINGS   PREP TIME: 5 MIN   COOKING TIME: 10 MIN

Crunchy outside, soft inside, lightly sweetened with a dash of cinnamon. These come together quickly and will be everyone's new favorite if they aren't already!

Ingredients

- 4 slices texas toast thick sliced bread
- 2 egg yolks
- 1/2 c milk
- 3 tbs sugar
- 1 tsp vanilla extract
- 1/2 c flour
- 1 1/2 tsp baking powder
- 1 1/2 tsp cinnamon
- 1/4 tsp salt
- oil for frying
- confectioner's sugar, for garnish
- maple syrup if desired

Directions

1. Slice each piece of bread into thirds.
2. In a mixing bowl, rapidly whisk the egg yolks, milk, and vanilla together until foamy.
3. Add the sugar to the bowl and whisk til dissolved.
4. In a separate bowl, mix the rest of the dry ingredients: flour, baking powder, cinnamon, and salt.
5. Mix the dry ingredients into the bowl with wet ingredients just until combined. Be careful not to over mix!
6. In a sauce pan or small frying pan, heat about 1-2 inches of oil over medium heat.
7. Test to see if the oil is ready by putting 1 drop of batter into the oil. If it immediately sizzles and floats, it is ready!
8. Take one cut section of bread and lightly coat it with with batter. It should not be saturated through, just coated outside. Scrape off any excess using the side of the bowl before gently placing it into the hot oil.
9. Repeat step 8, only frying a few at a time to avoid cooling the oil too rapidly or over-crowding the pan.
10. Fry each side for 2-3 minutes, or until browned.
11. Remove fried pieces from the pan and place on a paper-towel lined dish, or onto a cooling rack with a paper towel under it to preserve maximum crunchiness.
12. Repeat with the rest of the bread.
13. Once all pieces have been fried, plate them and dust the tops with a sprinkle of confectioner's sugar, and serve with (or without) maple syrup.

HANDHELDS

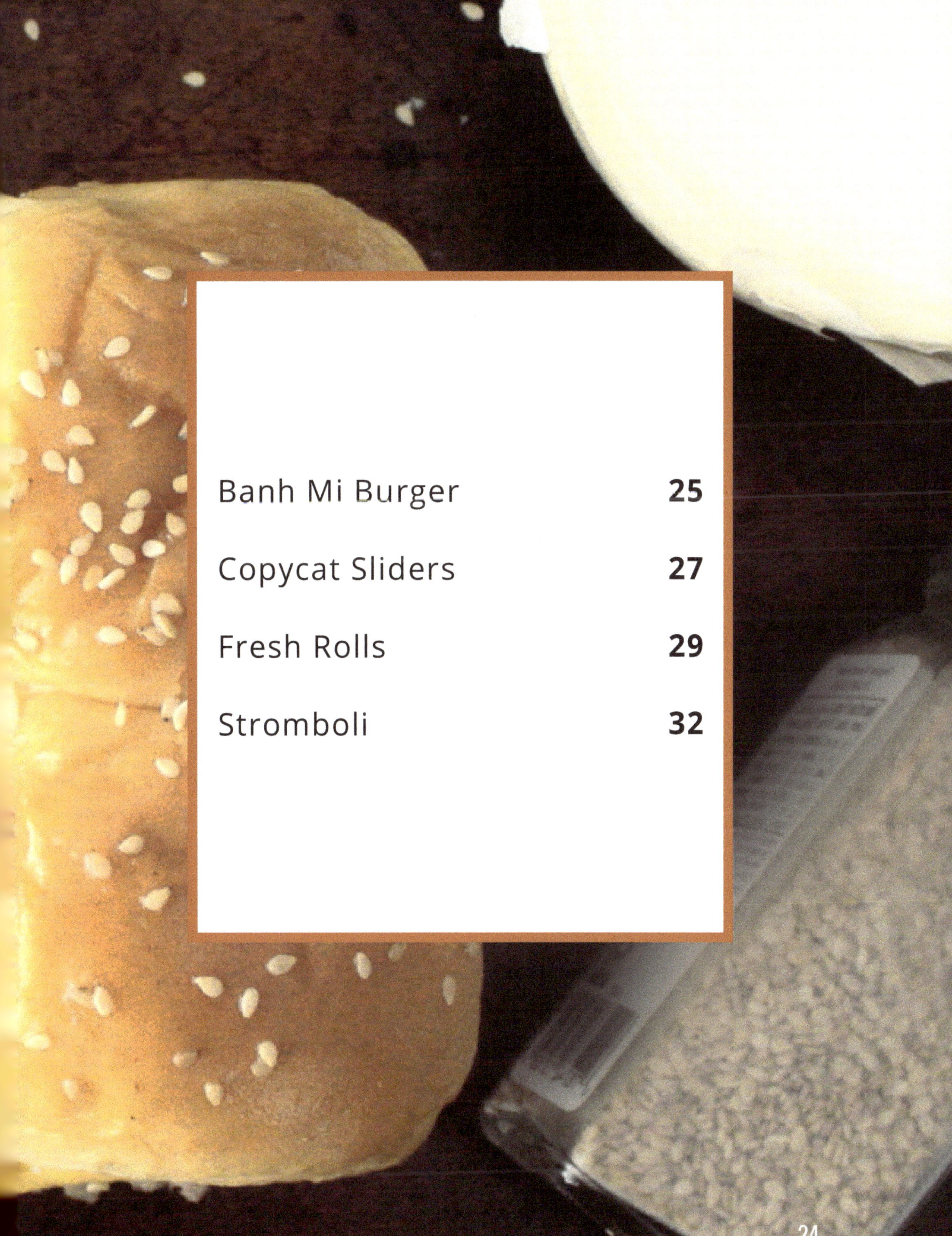

BANH MI BURGER

YIELD: 4 BURGERS PREP TIME: 20 MIN COOKING TIME: 10 MIN

Ingredients

Pickled Slaw:

- 1/2 c matchstick carrots
- 1/2 c thinly sliced cucumber
- 1 tbs chopped cilantro
- 3 tbs seasoned rice vinegar
- 1 tsp sugar

Burger mix:

- 1 lb ground pork
- 2 tbs mayo
- Sriracha to taste
- 3 cloves minced garlic
- 1 tsp fish sauce
- 1/2 tsp sesame oil
- 2 tbs chopped cilantro
- salt and pepper

Spicy mayo:

- 1/4 c mayo
- ssiracha to taste
- salt + pepper
- scallions

4 bulkie rolls, lightly toasted

Directions

1. Start by mixing all ingredients for the pickled slaw together in a small bowl. Cover and set aside until you're ready to assemble!
2. Mix the ingredients for the spicy mayo together and set aside as well.
3. In a large bowl, combine ingredients for the burger mix with your hands until well incorporated. Split the mix into four equal parts and form your burger patties.
4. Lightly coat a nonstick pan with oil over medium heat. Cook burgers about 6-8 minutes on each side or until internal temp reads 160 F. You can grill these if you prefer.
5. Assemble your burgers! Spread tops and bottoms of each toasted roll with the spicy mayo, layer on the burger patty and top each one with 1/4 of the pickled slaw. Add lettuce or other veggies if you desire, and serve!

use a wide-mouth mason jar ring or similar, lined with plastic wrap to form the burger patties so they are uniform in size and cook at the same rate.

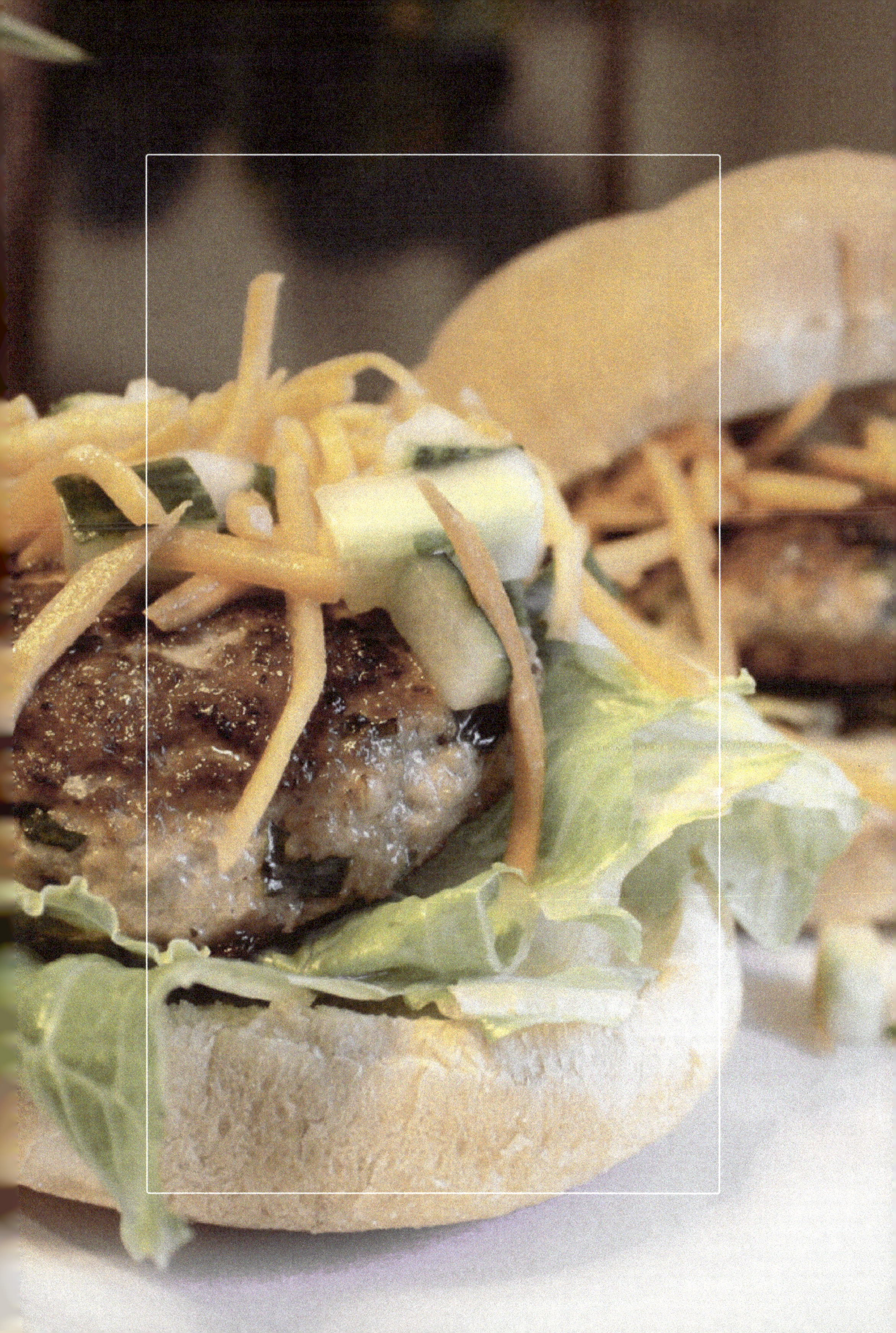

COPYCAT SLIDERS

YIELD: 12 SERVINGS   PREP TIME: 20 MIN   COOKING TIME: 25 MIN

A game day go-to that is easy to make for a crowd or just when that fast food craving hits.

Ingredients

- 1 12-pack of king's hawaiian original hawaiian sweet rolls
- 3 lb lean ground beef
- 1/2 c finely diced white onion
- 2 tbs seasoned salt
- garlic + onion powder
- 1/2 c thousand island dressing
- 10-12 slices of yellow american cheese
- dill relish or dill pickle slices to taste
- shredded lettuce (optional)

Directions

1. Preheat oven to 375 F.
2. While preheating, mix half of the finely diced onions into the raw ground beef.
3. Butter the bottom of 2 cookie sheets (with a rim/edge) and press and distribute half of the ground beef into an even layer on each.
4. Sprinkle the ground beef liberally with seasoned salt, garlic powder, onion powder, and the remaining onion. Bake at 375 F for 15 minutes or until the juices on the top run clear.
5. While the meat is cooking, slice the tops off of the rolls and spread thousand island dressing on the tops, and dill relish or pickles on the bottom bun.
6. When beef is cooked through, cover the top with slices of cheese, and put back in the oven until cheese is melted.
7. Carefully place the cooked meat on the bottom buns, trim to fit as needed, and place the tops of the buns over the meat.
8. Brush the tops of the buns with melted butter and sprinkle with white sesame seeds if desired.
9. Cut along the perforations of the rolls and serve.

not a 'mac fan? sub in any toppings that you prefer on your favorite burger. bacon, lettuce, tomatoes, etc! keep it as simple or as wild as you like.

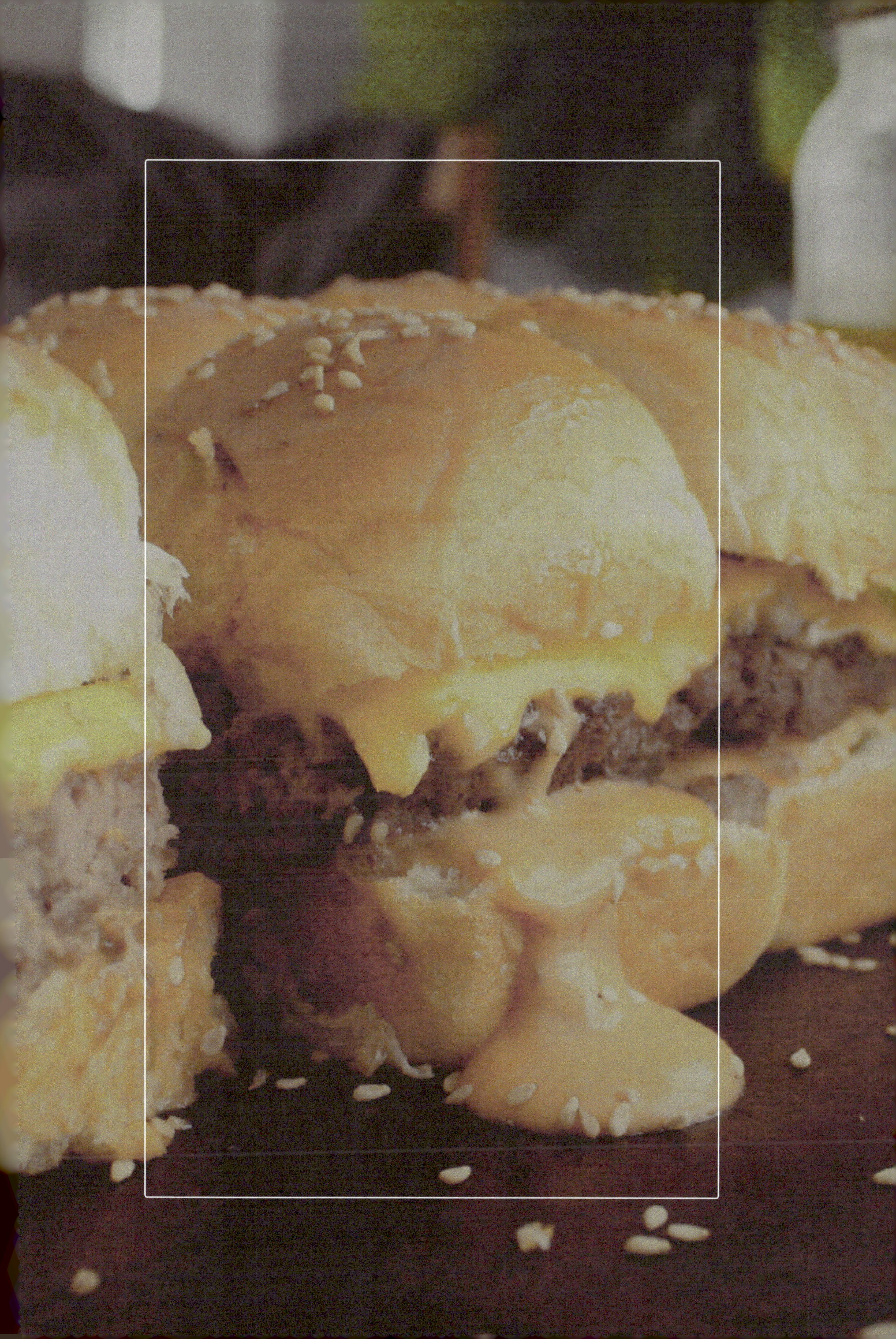

SUMMER ROLLS

YIELD: 6-8 ROLLS PREP TIME: 10 MIN COOKING TIME: 5 MIN

A spin on one of my family's favorites. We were introduced to Vietnamese Fresh Rolls by my aunt and uncle's foreign exchange student, Duc, and these have been a staple since! These may not be "traditional" fresh rolls but are so versatile and of course, fresh and delicious!

Ingredients

- round rice paper wrappers
- 1 english cucumber, cut into sticks
- 1 c matchstick carrots
- 3 c shredded lettuce or cabbage
- 2 c bean sprouts
- chopped cilantro or basil
- 1 bunch of green onions, chopped
- 1 c cooked, shredded chicken (or tofu, shrimp, etc)

peanut sauce

- 1/2 c peanut butter
- 1/4 c soy sauce
- 2 tbs sesame oil
- 2 tbs rice vinegar
- 2 tbs chili paste/sriracha (to taste)
- 1/4 c honey
- 1 tsp ground ginger
- 2 cloves minced garlic
- water as needed to thin

Directions

1. Cook and the chicken (or shred up a rotisserie) and boil the rice noodles according to package instruction.
2. Choose and chop all the veggies you wish to use for your fillings, you can add in or leave out anything, and it will still be delicious
3. Arrange your desired filling selections in sections around a platter for a DIY summer roll experience.
4. Make the peanut sauce! Add all ingredients except water to a bowl or a food processor and whisk or pulse until it is smooth.
5. Add water by the teaspoon as needed for desired consistency. I prefer mine a little sweet and spicy, so sometimes I'll add in a little extra brown sugar and chili paste. Experiment with flavors you enjoy!
6. Assemble the rolls: fill a shallow dish with cool water and dip in the rice paper to wet the entire surface.
7. Lay the paper on a plastic or wooden cutting board, and it will quickly soften. Layer the center of the rice paper with any veggies and proteins you like, as well as the rice noodles
8. Roll it up like a burrito! Tuck the side closest to you over the fillings, wrap the two outer sides in toward the center, and finally roll up the wrap.
9. Dip the roll into the peanut sauce and enjoy!

easily adapted for vegan/vegetarian diets, and if you use tamari instead of soy sauce, the sauce can be gluten free too!

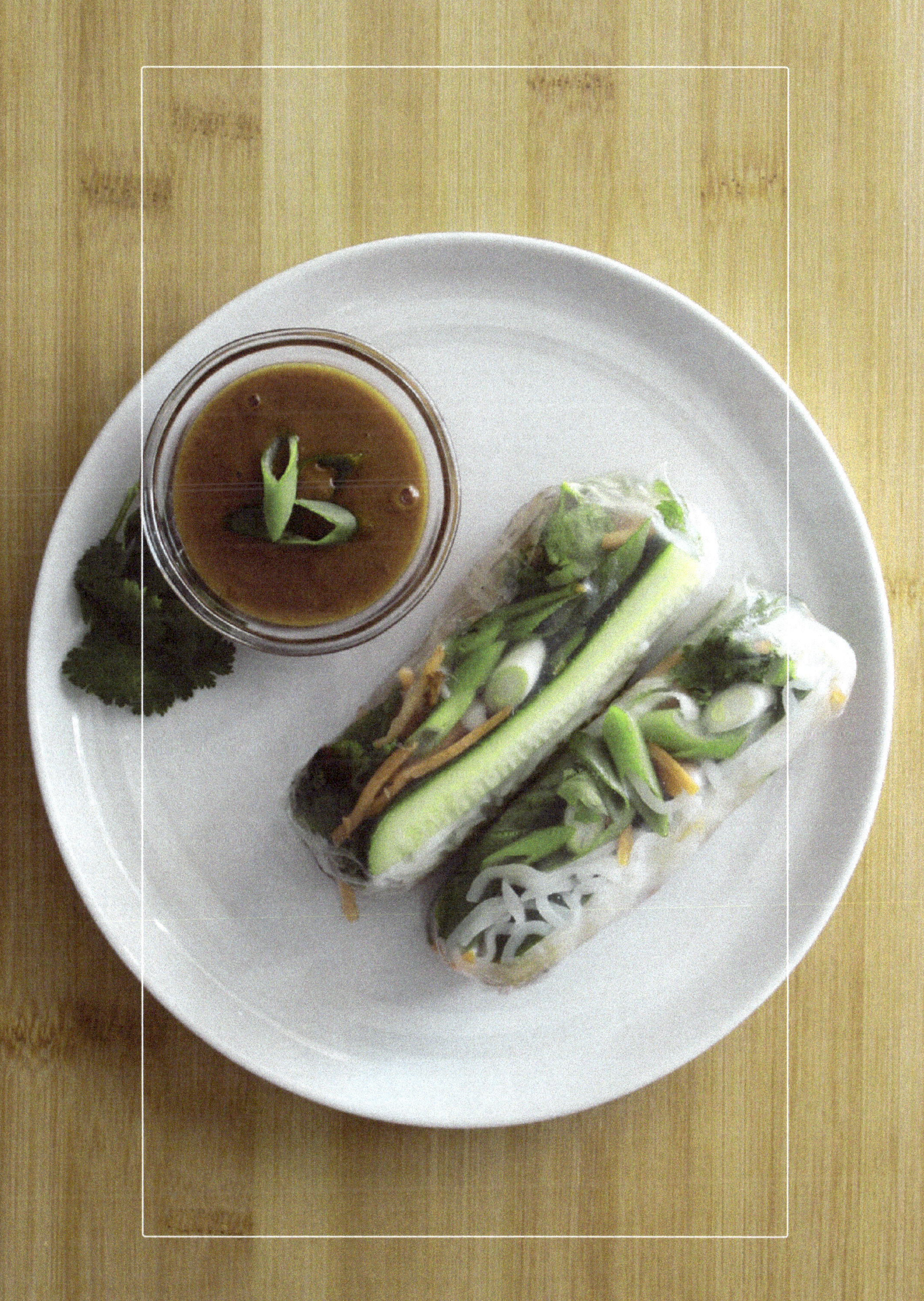

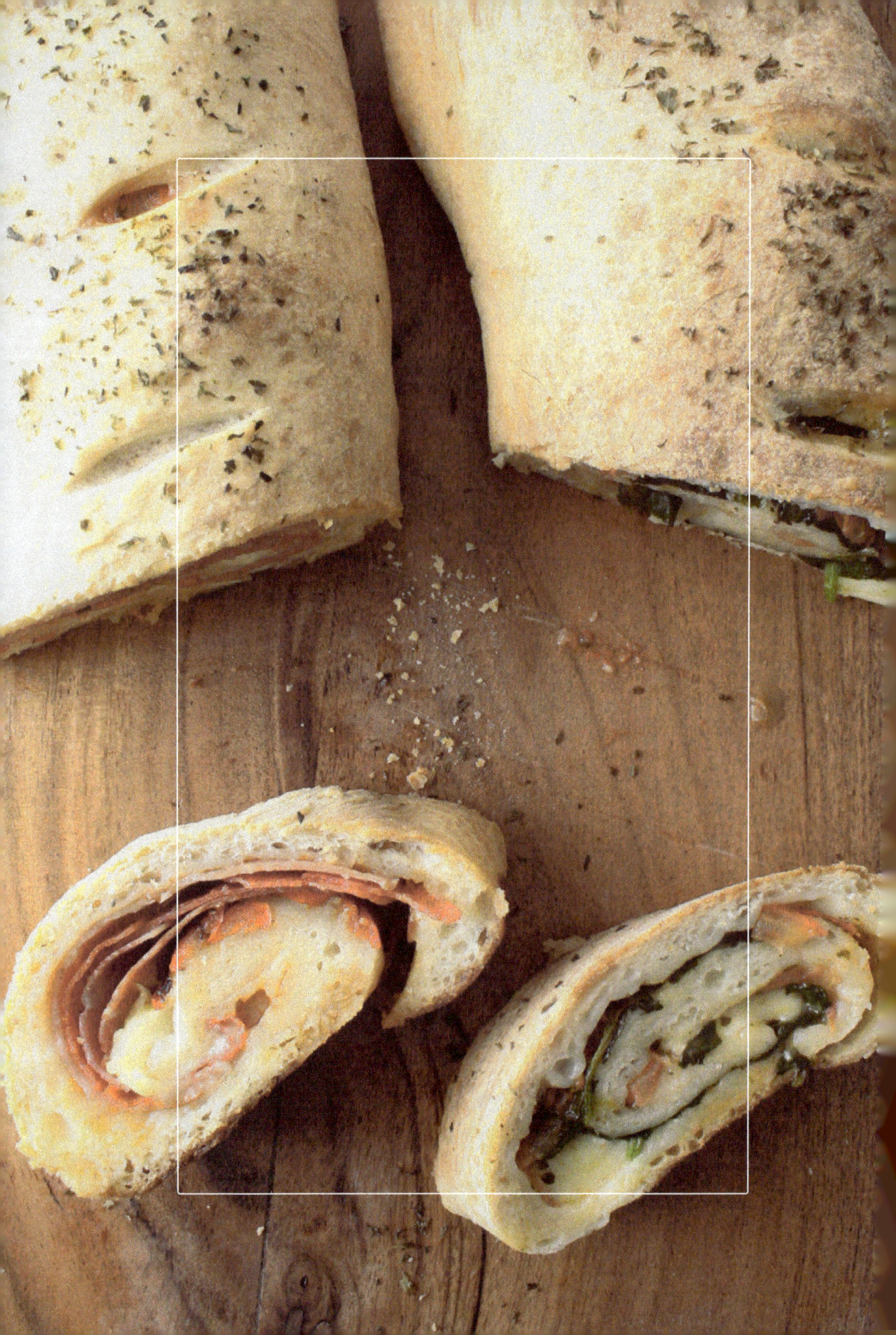

STROMBOLI

YIELD: 1 STROMBOLI   PREP TIME: 10 MIN   COOKING TIME: 25-30 MIN

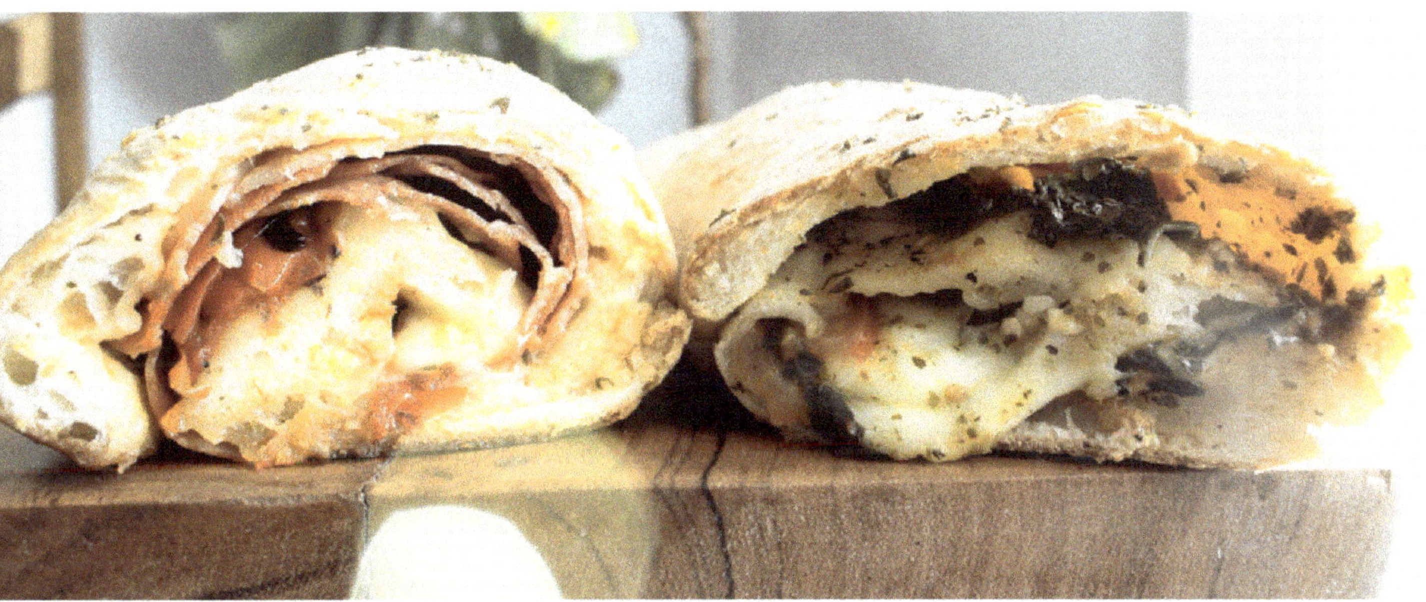

Ingredients

- 1 lb pizza dough
- 1/4 c pizza sauce plus more for dipping
- 4 oz mozzarella
- your favorite pizza toppings
- 3 tbs melted butter
- dried basil and parsley

Directions

1. Preheat oven to 375 F.
2. On a floured surface, roll out the pizza dough into a large rectangle shape.
3. Spread the dough lightly with pizza sauce, sprinkle with cheese, and add any of your favorite toppings. For mine pictured, I used salami, pepperoni, ham, and sauteed red peppers in one, and pesto, mozzarella and spinach in the other.
4. From the long edge closest to you, roll the dough and fillings into a log shape.
5. Stretch and tuck the outer edges under the log and pinch to ensure a good seal along the bottom seam as well as the sides.
6. Brush the top with olive oil or melted butter and sprinkle some basil and parsely on top.
7. With a very sharp knife, create 4-5 small slices in the top of the log to allow steam to escape.
8. Transfer gently to a parchment lined baking sheet with seam-side down, and bake for 25-30 minutes or until golden brown.

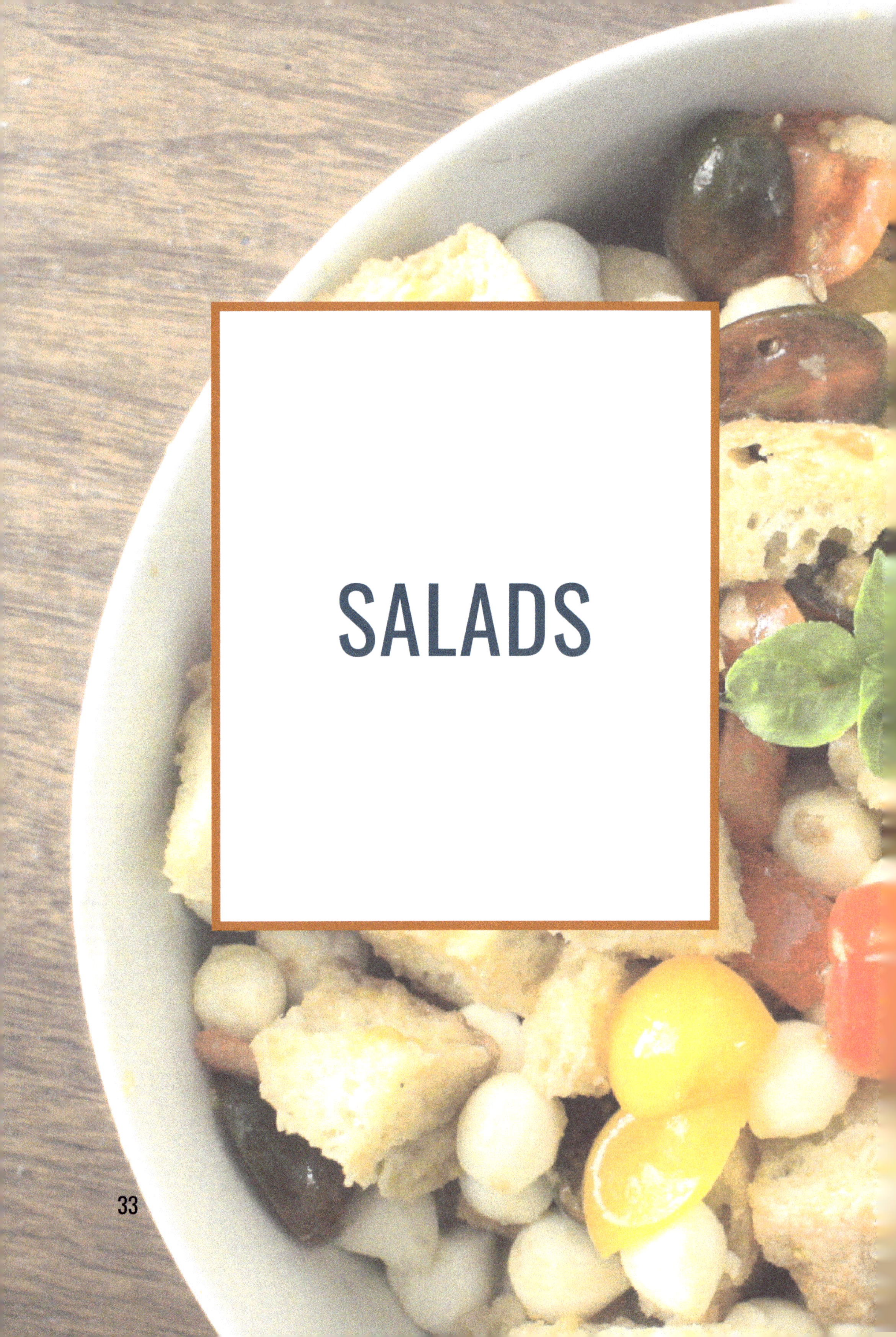

SALADS

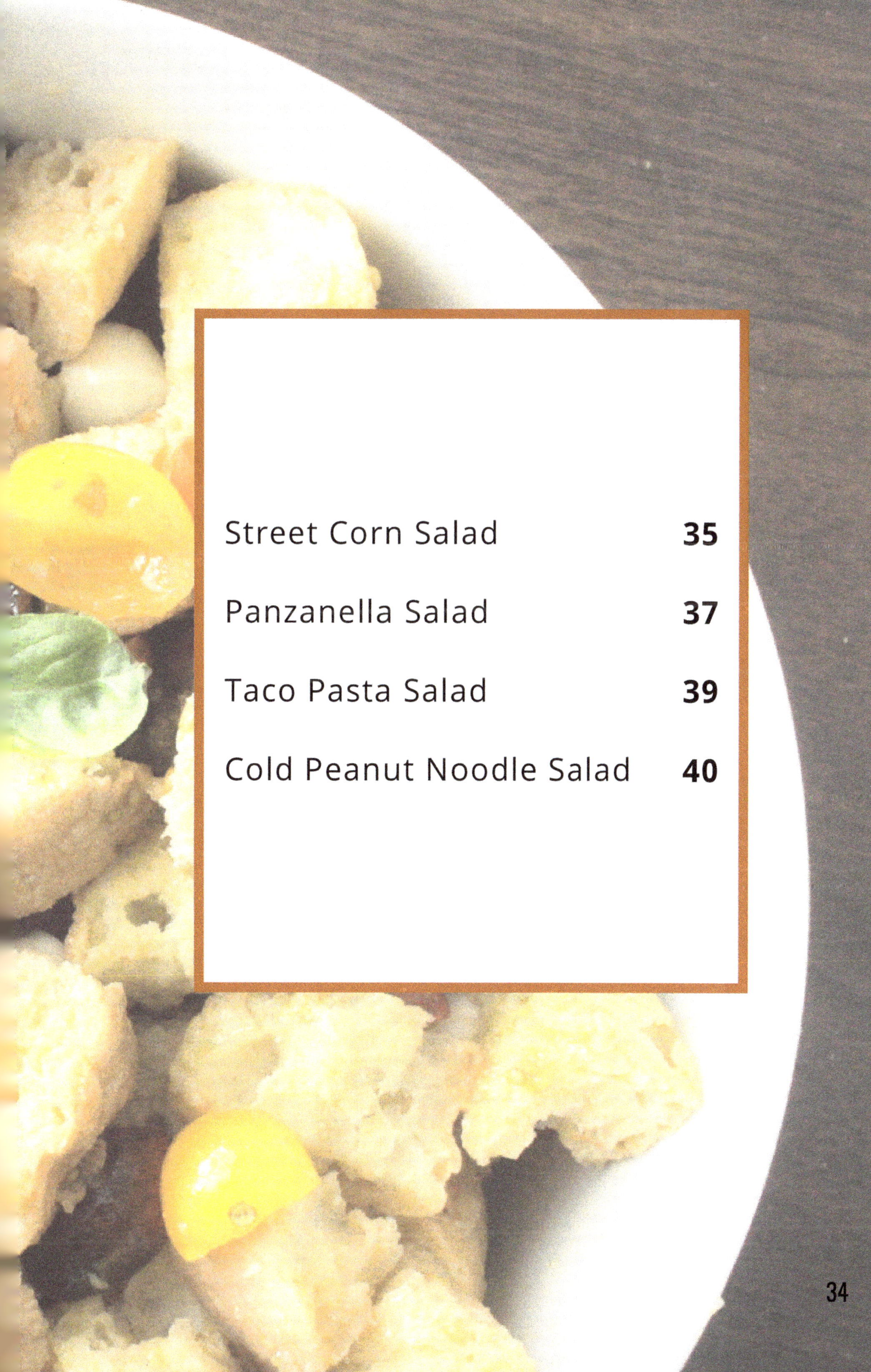

STREET CORN SALAD

YIELD: 8-10 SERVINGS   PREP TIME: 10 MIN   COOKING TIME: 10 MIN

Ingredients

- 2 bags of frozen corn
- 1 bag of frozen chopped onions
- 1/2 english cucumber, diced
- 2 c halved cherry or grape tomatoes
- cilantro to taste
- 2 tsp each salt and pepper
- 1 tsp onion powder
- 1 tsp garlic powder
- juice of 1 lime
- 1/2 block of cotija cheese, crumbled
- chili powder and cumin to taste, or use Tajin seasoning

Directions

1. In a dry, hot pan, char the corn and onions in batches on medium-high until they lose some moisture and have spots of brown or black. They don't need to be burned to a crisp, just a little color. Remove from pan and let cool.
2. Dice half an english cucumber, and slice the cherry tomatoes in half.
3. Once the corn and onions are lighly charred and cooled, combine in a large bowl with the cucumbers and tomatoes. You may like to add some of the crumbled cotija in the salad as well.
4. Mix in the cilantro if desired, as well as the salt, pepper, garlic and onion powder.
5. If using Tajin or chili powder and cumin, add that in too.
6. Squeeze the juice of a cut lime over everything and mix well to combine.
7. Top with crumbled cotija (also known as queso fresco), and chill before serving.

another easy substitute for this salad is any mexican/southwest style salad dressing you prefer! if using, mix that in first before you add any seasonings to the salad. i've used Bolthouse Farms Cilantro-Avocado Yogurt dressing with great success!

can't find cotija? feta works just fine in a pinch. don't be afraid to add more of what you do like, and feel free to omit what you don't!

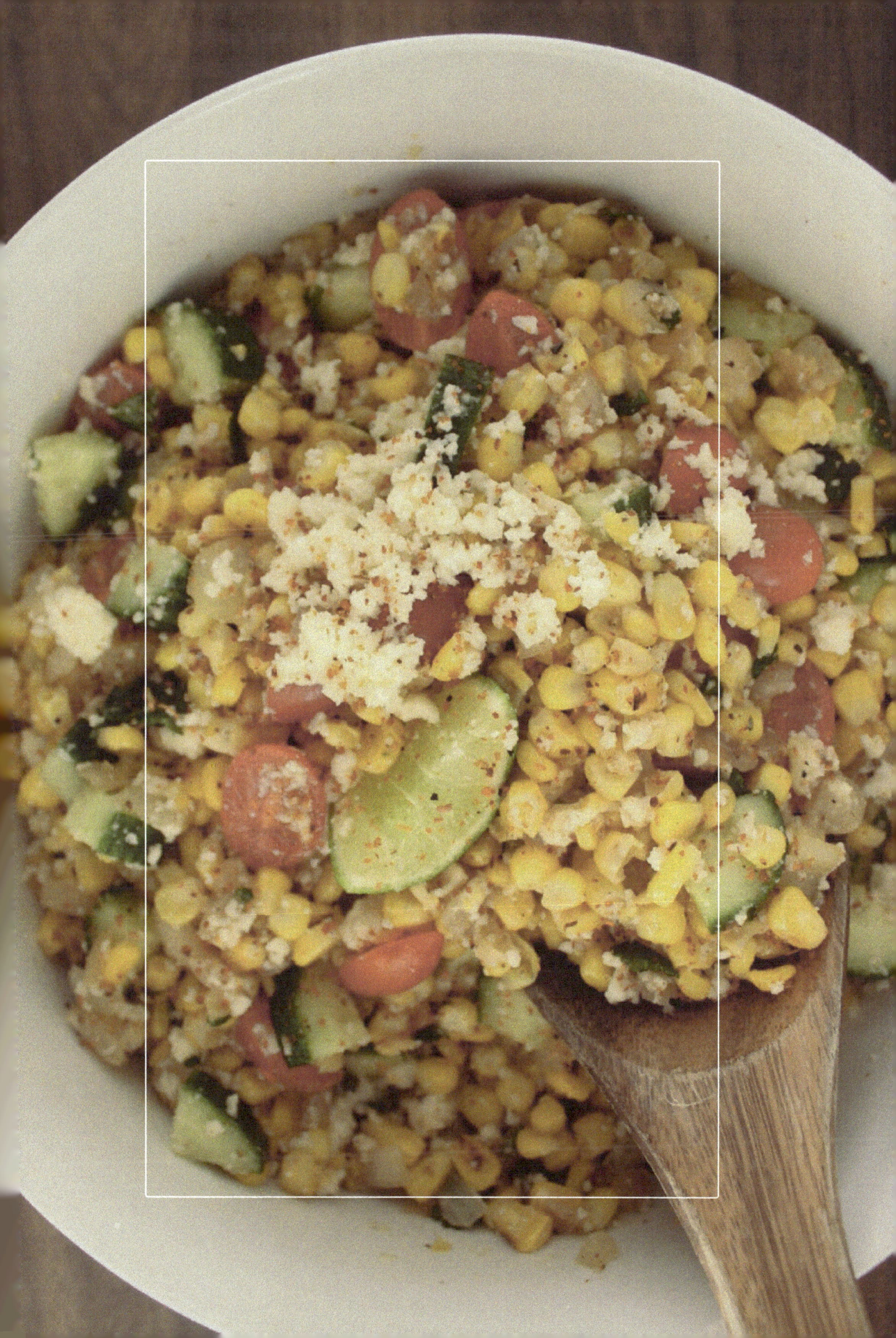

PANZANELLA SALAD

YIELD: 6-8 SERVINGS PREP TIME: 30 MIN WAIT TIME: 30 MIN

A fresh, tangy and delicious way to use up the last tomatoes of summer. Plus. it's a "salad" so its good for you even though its 90% bread, right?

Ingredients

- 1 lb heirloom cherry tomatoes, sliced in half
- 2 tbs salt
- 6 c cubed fresh ciabatta bread
- 1 lb container mozzarella pearls
- 1/2 c olive oil
- 3 cloves garlic, minced
- 2 tbs chopped white onion
- 1/2 tsp mustard
- 2 tbs red wine vinegar
- black pepper, fresh basil to taste

Directions

1. Preheat oven to 350 F.
2. Place a colander over a bowl of a similar size and pour in the sliced tomatoes.
3. Sprinkle the salt over the tomatoes and mix well. Let the juices drain into the bowl for 15-20 minutes.
4. Arrange the bread cubes on a baking sheet and lightly drizzle with some olive oil. Place in the oven and bake, turning once halfway, for 15 minutes. The bread should be soft on the inside with a crunchy but not browned outside.
5. Remove the colander from the bowl with the tomato juice; but do not toss out those tasty tomato juices!!
6. To the tomato juice, add in the rest of the olive oil, garlic, onion, mustard, and red wine vinegar. whisk quickly and constantly to combine all ingredients.
7. In a separate bowl. combine the toasted bread cubes, tomatoes and mozzarella pearls.
8. Toss the bread and tomato mixture with the dressing and let it all rest together for 30 minutes so the bread absorbs the delicious tomato flavor of the vinaigrette.
9. Add an optional drizzle of balsamic glaze for an appetizing splash of color and flavor right before serving.

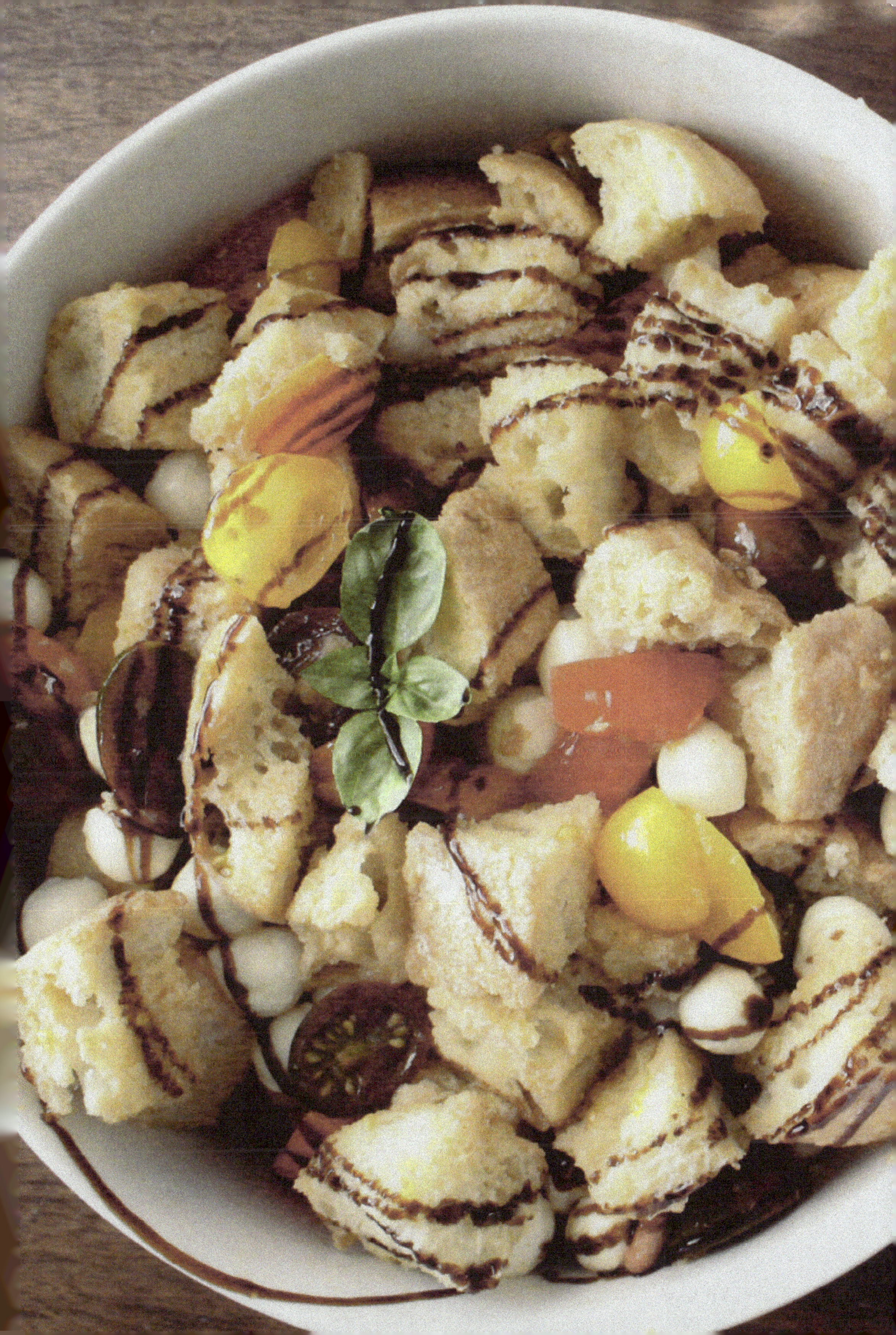

TACO PASTA SALAD

YIELD: 4-6 SERVINGS   PREP TIME: 20 MIN   COOKING TIME: 10 MIN

You'll never look at taco night leftovers the same again.

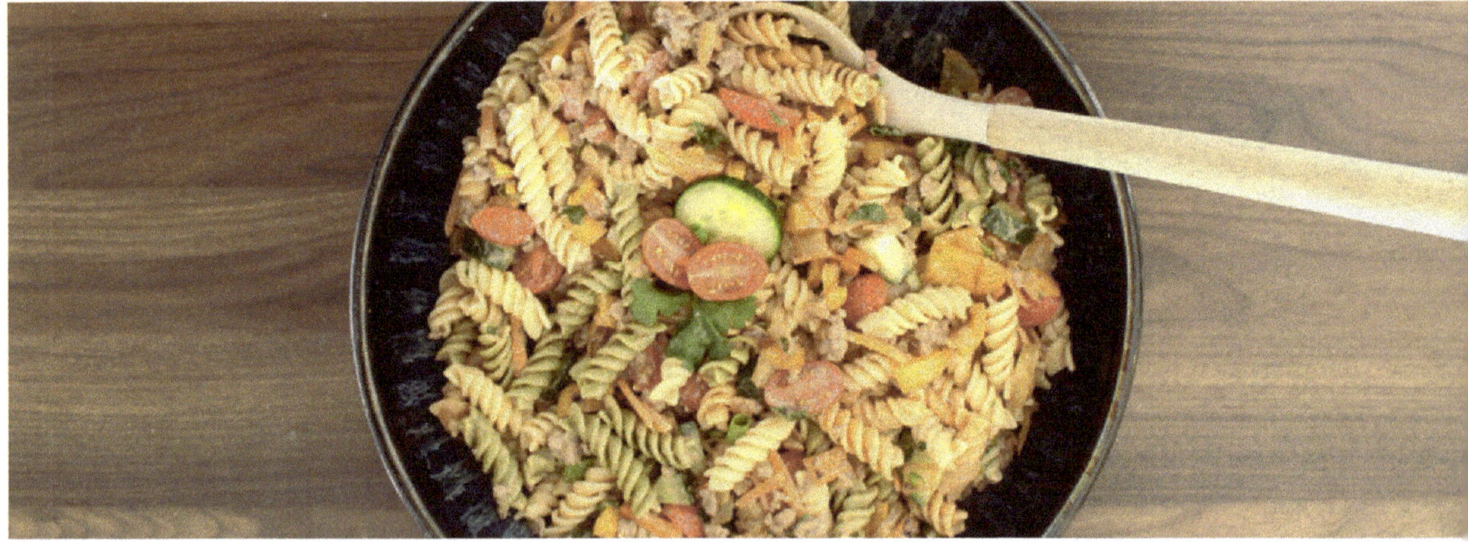

Ingredients

- 1 lb rotini pasta, cooked, drained and cooled
- 1 yellow pepper, diced
- 1/2 sweet onion, diced
- 1 c matchstick carrots
- 1/2 english cucumber, diced
- 1 c halved cherry or grape tomatoes
- 1/2 c salsa
- 1/2 c sour cream
- 1 tsp garlic powder
- 1 tsp onion powder
- 1/2 packet of ranch seasoning mix
- 2 c cooked taco beef

Directions

1. Cook the pasta according to package instructions, drain, and rinse with cold water.
2. Dice the pepper and onion, and toss into a pan on medium high heat to slightly char and caramelize the veggies, stirring once, for about 5 minutes. Once done, remove from the pan and allow to cool.
3. Place the carrots, diced cucumber, and halved tomatoes into a large bowl, add in the taco meat (left overs work perfectly, or cook it up and cool it prior to this step), pasta, peppers and onions.
4. Mix together the dressing; combine salsa, sour cream, and ranch seasoning til smooth. Pour over the veggies, meat, and pasta and mix to coat all of the bits.
5. Add cilantro if desired, and enjoy right away.

to freshen up leftover salad, add in some mayo or mix up more of the sour cream and salsa dressing.

COLD PEANUT NOODLE SALAD

YIELD: 6-8 SERVINGS PREP TIME: 10 MIN COOKING TIME: 15 MIN

Ingredients

- 1 lb spaghetti
- 1/2 english cucumber, diced
- 1 cup chopped romaine lettuce
- 1 c matchstick carrots
- 3 tbs chopped fresh cilantro
- 1 bunch scallions, sliced
- sesame seeds to garnish
- 1/2 lb chicken tenderloins, chopped
- 1/2 c soy sauce
- 3 cloves garlic, minced

peanut sauce

- 1/2 c peanut butter
- 1/4 c soy sauce
- 2 tbs sesame oil
- 2 tbs rice vinegar
- 2 tbs chili paste/sriracha (to taste)
- 1/4 c honey
- 1 tsp ground ginger
- 2 cloves minced garlic
- water as needed to thin

Directions

1. Marinate the chicken in 1/2 c soy sauce for 30 minutes. Saute in a pan over medium-high heat with the soy sauce and 3 cloves of minced garlic until cooked through, and set aside to cool.
2. Boil spaghetti per package instructions, drain, and rinse with cold water.
3. Prepare vegetables, and place in a large bowl with the pasta and the cooked chicken.
4. Make the peanut sauce! Add all ingredients except water to a bowl or a food processor and whisk or pulse until it is smooth. Add water as needed until desired consistency is reached.
5. Add water 1 tsp at a time if sauce needs thinning.
6. Pour the peanut sauce over the noodles and veggies in the large bowl and toss to coat evenly.

i recommend dressing this right before serving! the noodles soak up the sauce if mixed together more than a few hours in advance. you could always make extra sauce for later, too- you'll probably want to put it on everything.

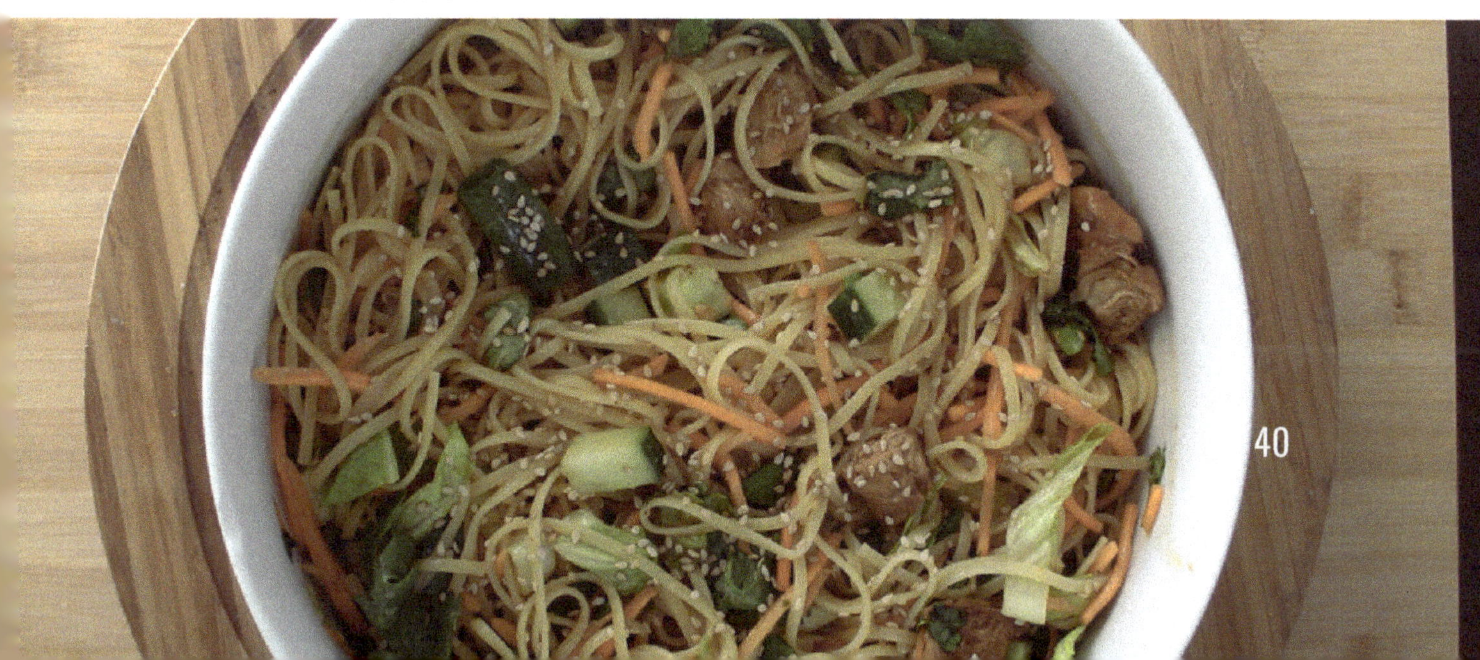

SOUPS + STEWS

HEARTY HOMESTYLE CHILI

YIELD: 6-8 SERVINGS   PREP TIME:15 MIN   COOKING TIME: 25+ MIN

I find a lot of people make chili with a tex-mex flair or taco-like flavors... Not here though. This chili will warm you to the core and is perfect for either the crock pot or stove top method.

Ingredients

- 1 yellow onion
- 3 tbs minced garlic
- 1 bell pepper
- 1 tbs whiskey (optional)
- 1/2 a 6oz can of tomato paste
- 1 lb ground beef or alternative
- 1/3 c BBQ sauce
- 2 c frozen corn kernels
- 1 can black beans, rinsed
- 1 can red beans, rinsed
- 2 14 1/2 oz cans petite diced tomatoes, drained
- 1 28oz can crushed tomatoes
- salt, pepper, chili powder, oregano, paprika, parsley

Directions

1. In a pan over medium heat, cook onions, garlic and peppers until fragrant. (If making this on the stove top, use your stock pot/soup pot for this step to make it a 1-pot meal)
2. Add in ground beef and season liberally with salt, pepper, chili powder, oregano, paprika, and parsley flakes. Break up the beef while browning.
3. When the beef is just about done, add in 3 oz (1/2 can) of tomato paste and 1/3 cup of BBQ sauce and mix in thoroughly.
4. If using a crock pot, transfer the beef mixture to the crock pot now. If you're cooking in a large stock pot on the stove, skip to step 5.
5. Add the rest of the canned ingredients to the pot and mix to combine.
6. Keep over low heat for as long as you can stand to wait, at least until hot. Don't forget to give it a taste and add more seasonings if needed.
7. Serve with a sprinkle of cheese or a dollop of sour cream, or with a piece of cornbread.

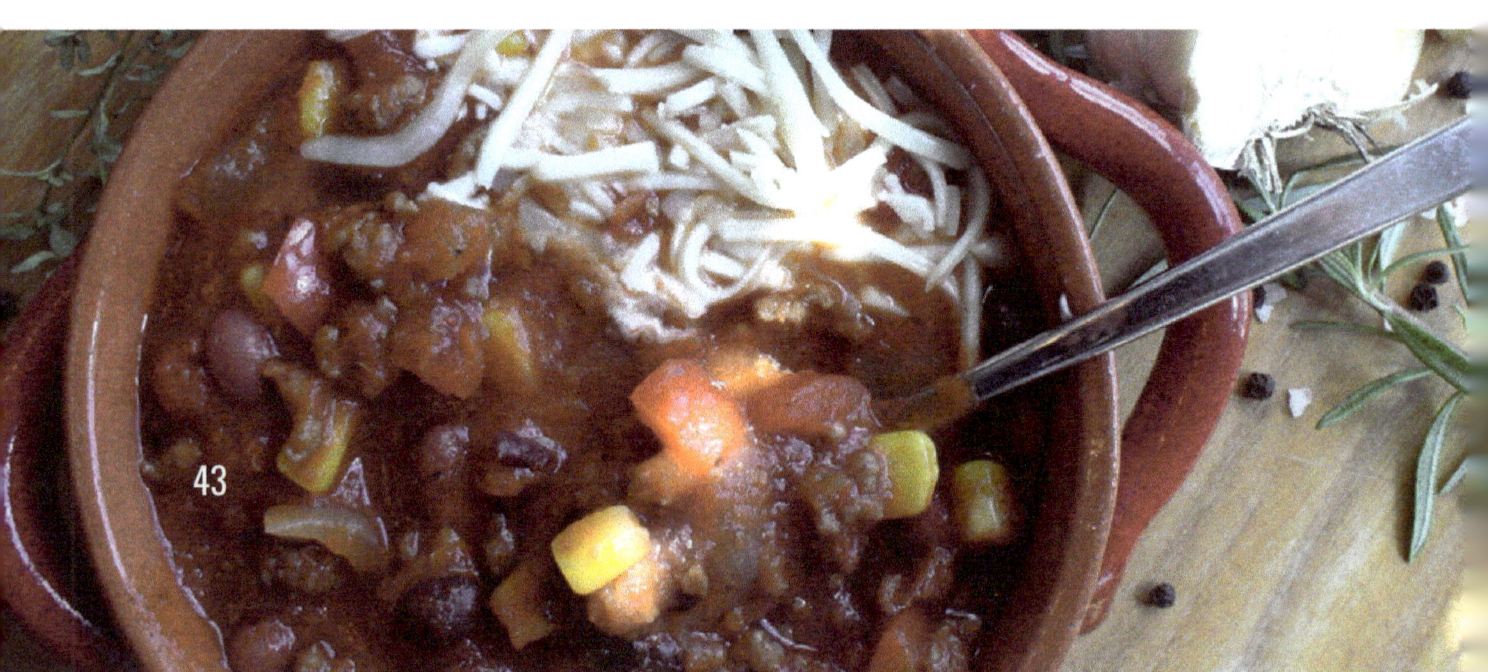

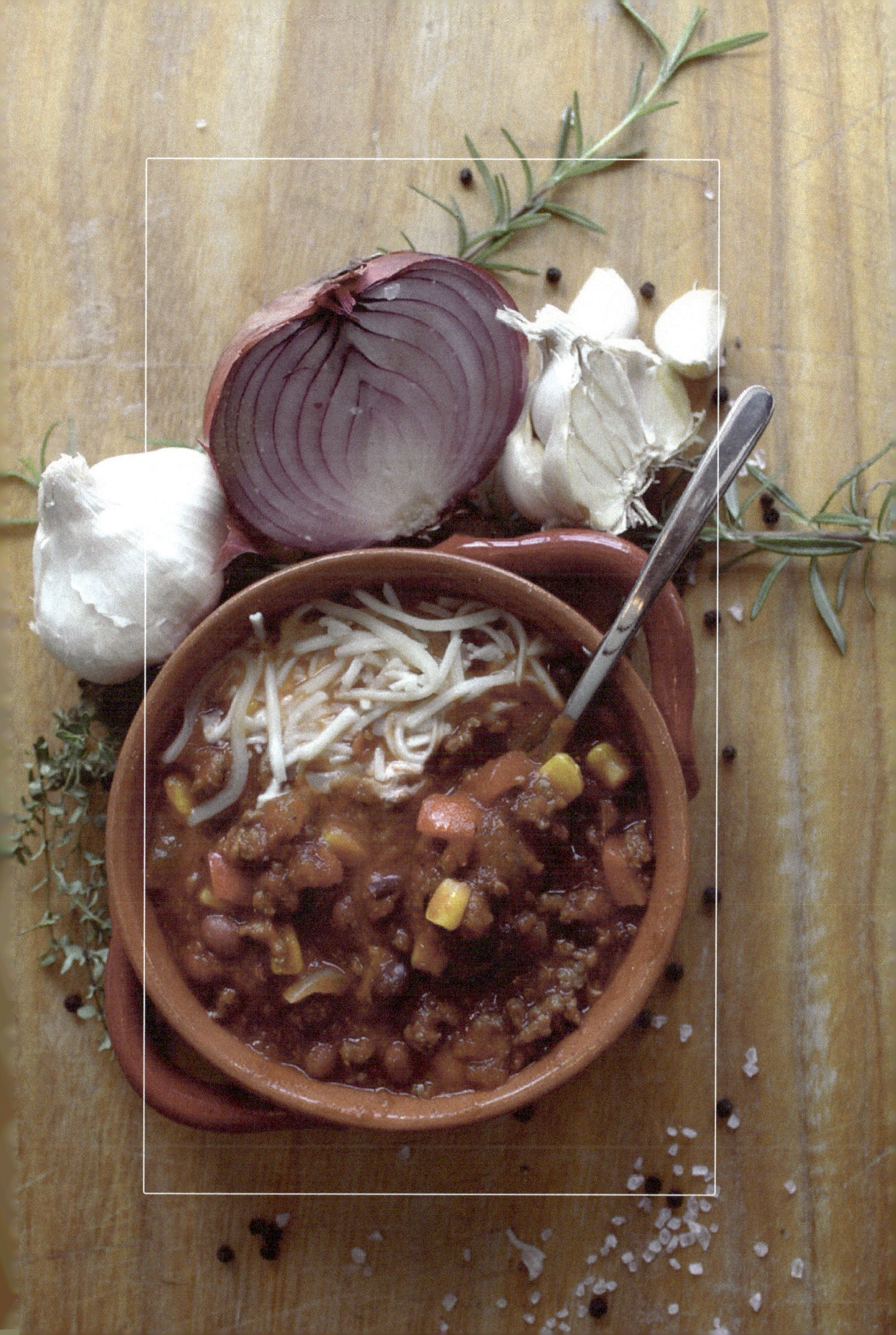

HARVEST SQUASH SOUP

YIELD: 10 SERVINGS PREP TIME: 10 MIN COOKING TIME: 45 MIN

The flavors of fall are front and center in this velvety smooth, sweet and savory soup.

Ingredients

- 1 lb butterut squash, halved, cleaned, peeled and cut into chunks
- 1 large acorn squash, halved and cleaned
- 1 sweet potato, peeled and cut
- 1 red potato, peeled and cut
- 1 c baby carrots
- 3 cloves of garlic, minced
- 1 white onion
- 1 apple, peeled cored and cut
- almond milk
- 2- 32 oz containers of vegetable broth
- 1 tsp each salt, pepper, thyme, ginger, cinnamon, nutmeg, or to taste
- 1/4 tsp yellow curry powder (optional, but recommended!)
- maple syrup or brown sugar to taste
- blender, immersion blender, or food processor

Directions

1. Preheat oven to 375 F and cut/prepare vegetables as indicated.
2. Place the acorn squash cut-side down on a lightly oiled baking sheet, poke holes with a fork or knife around the skin of the squash and roast for 45 minutes to an hour or until tender.
3. To a large stock pot add the vegetable stock and bring to a rolling boil.
4. Carefully add in the butternut squash, sweet potato, red potato, carrots, garlic, onion, and apple. Cook for 30-40 minutes or until all veggies are easily pierced with a fork.
5. Remove acorn squash from the oven and let cool before handling. Scoop out the flesh and add it to the pot .
6. Once all vegetables are soft, ladle the soup into the pitcher of your blender or food processor. Blend in batches on high speed until smooth, and set aside, repeating this process until you have pureed all of the contents of the stock pot.
7. Return the pureed soup to the pot. Over medium-low heat, bring it back to a gentle boil. Add almond milk little by little until you have reached your desired consistency.
8. Add in seasonings to taste. I would recommend starting with 1 tsp of each at the most, and building upon that until you get the flavor balance you like.
9. Mix in maple syrup or brown sugar 2 tbs at a time until desired sweetness is reached.

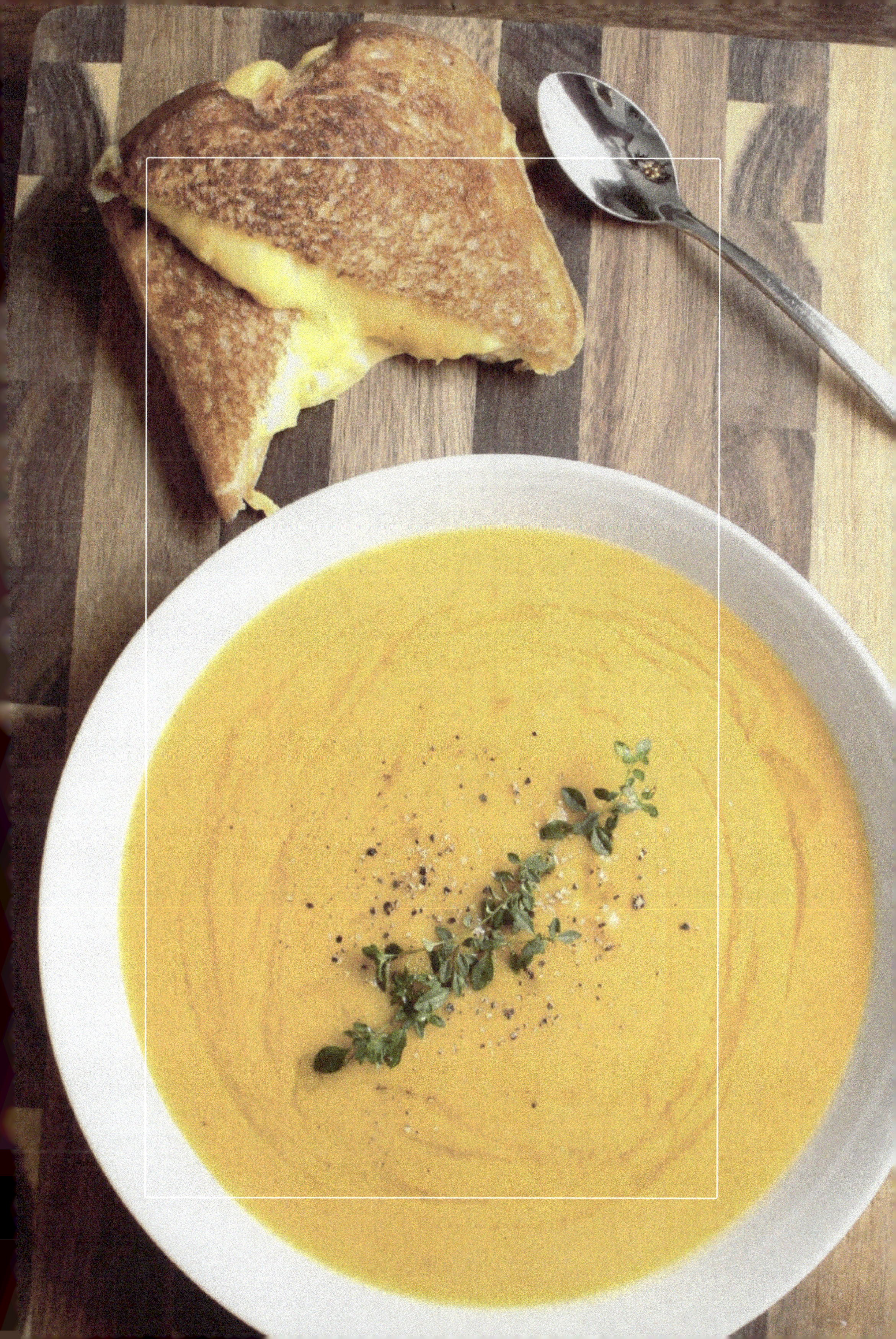

FRENCH ONION RAMEN

YIELD: 4-6 SERVINGS PREP TIME: 30 MIN COOKING TIME: 20 MIN

Umami meets a cozy classic with a hint of aromatics and spice.

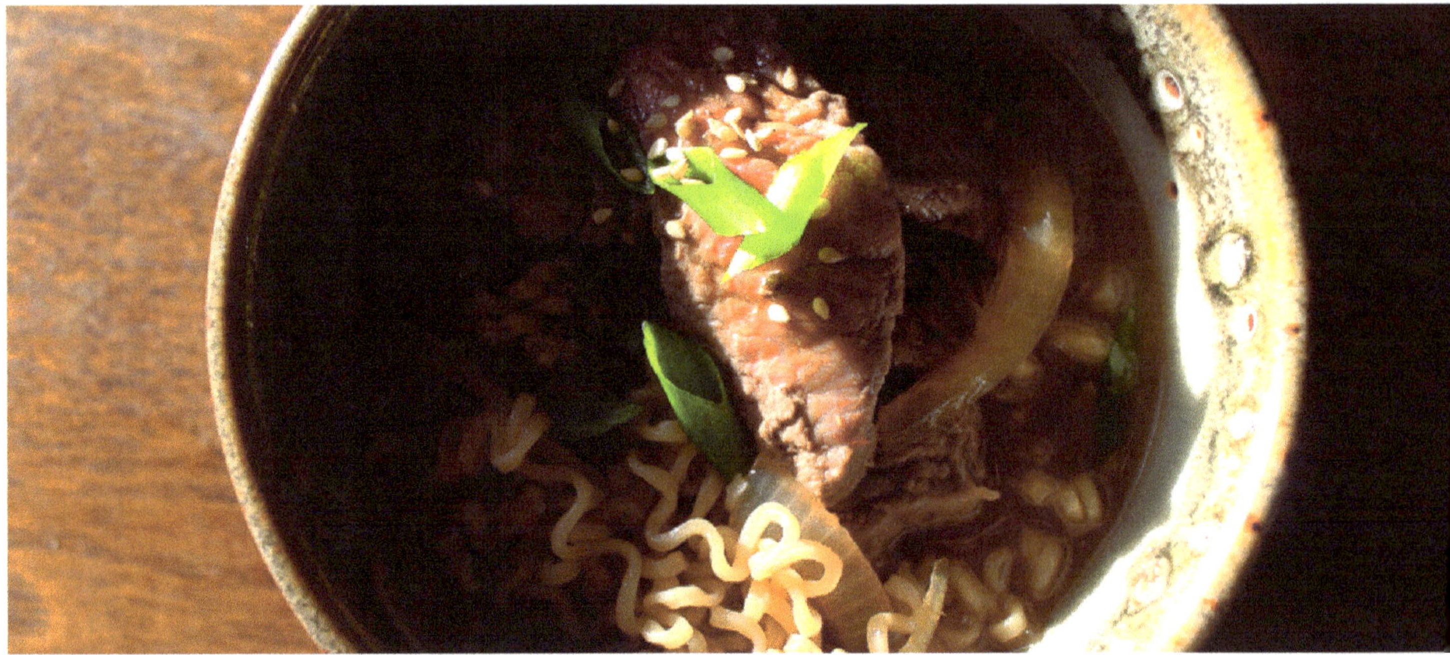

Ingredients

- 1 lb sirloin, cut into 1/2" slices
- 1/4 c soy sauce
- 3 tbs oil
- 1 tsp grated ginger
- 1/8 tsp red pepper flake
- 3 whole cloves
- 1/2 tsp thyme
- dusting of nutmeg
- 3 cloves garlic, minced
- 1 tbs rice vinegar
- 2 whole onions, finely sliced
- 6 c beef stock
- 1 c dry red wine
- 3 packs ramen noodles*

**in a pinch, you can boil spaghetti noodles with a tablespoon of baking soda to mimic the texture of ramen. In this case, cook them separately, drain + add to the serving bowl, then top with the broth.*

Directions

1. Marinate sliced beef in 1/4 c soy sauce for 30 minutes.
2. While beef is marinating, prepare the seasonings and thinly slice 2 onions.
3. Heat 3 tbs oil in a 4 qt pot over medium-high heat. Add in ginger, pepper flakes, cloves, thyme, nutmeg, and garlic.
4. Once the oil becomes aromatic, quickly sear only **one** side of each slice of steak, then remove from the pot and set aside. (Hot broth will continue to cook the steak when you serve it together!)
5. Reduce heat to medium-low, and add onions to the pot. Caramelize the onions for 10 minutes, stirring occasionally, until browned.
6. Stir in rice vinegar and wine to the onions, followed by the beef broth. Bring to a steady boil.
7. Place the ramen noodle bricks into the boiling broth and cook for 4-5 minutes or until 'al dente.'
8. Serve the soup topped with the sirloin and scallions.

LOADED CORN CHOWDER

YIELD: 6-8 SERVINGS PREP TIME: 20 MIN COOKING TIME: 45 MIN

Absolutely loaded with veggie goodness and bursting with flavor. If you thought Ma's corn chowder couldn't be better... think again.

Ingredients

- 1 c bacon, cooked, drained and chopped (about 8 slices)
- 1 yellow onion, diced
- 2 minced garlic cloves
- 1 c chopped celery
- 1 c chopped carrot
- 4 c diced red potatoes
- 4 c corn - fresh or frozen!
- 4 c veggie or chicken stock
- 2 tbs butter
- 2 c water
- 1 c heavy cream
- 1 block of medium cheddar, shredded
- 1/2 packet of ranch seasoning mix
- 1 tsp thyme
- tiny, tiny sprinkle of nutmeg

Directions

1. Put butter in a large stock pot over medium heat, add onion, garlic, celery, carrots and potatoes and cook until the onion is soft.
2. Pour in the stock and water, and mix in the ranch packet, thyme, corn and a tiny pinch of nutmeg.
3. Bring to a steady simmer and cook until potatoes are fork tender, about 8-10 minutes.
4. Slowly stir in the half and half or your creamy milk alternative and return to a simmer. Add in the bacon and shredded cheddar. It's best to use block cheddar that is hand-shredded since the bagged stuff has anti-caking agents which inhibits that smooth melt we love for soups especially.
5. Bring your soup back to a simmer for 20 minutes (or more) to reduce and thicken, then serve.

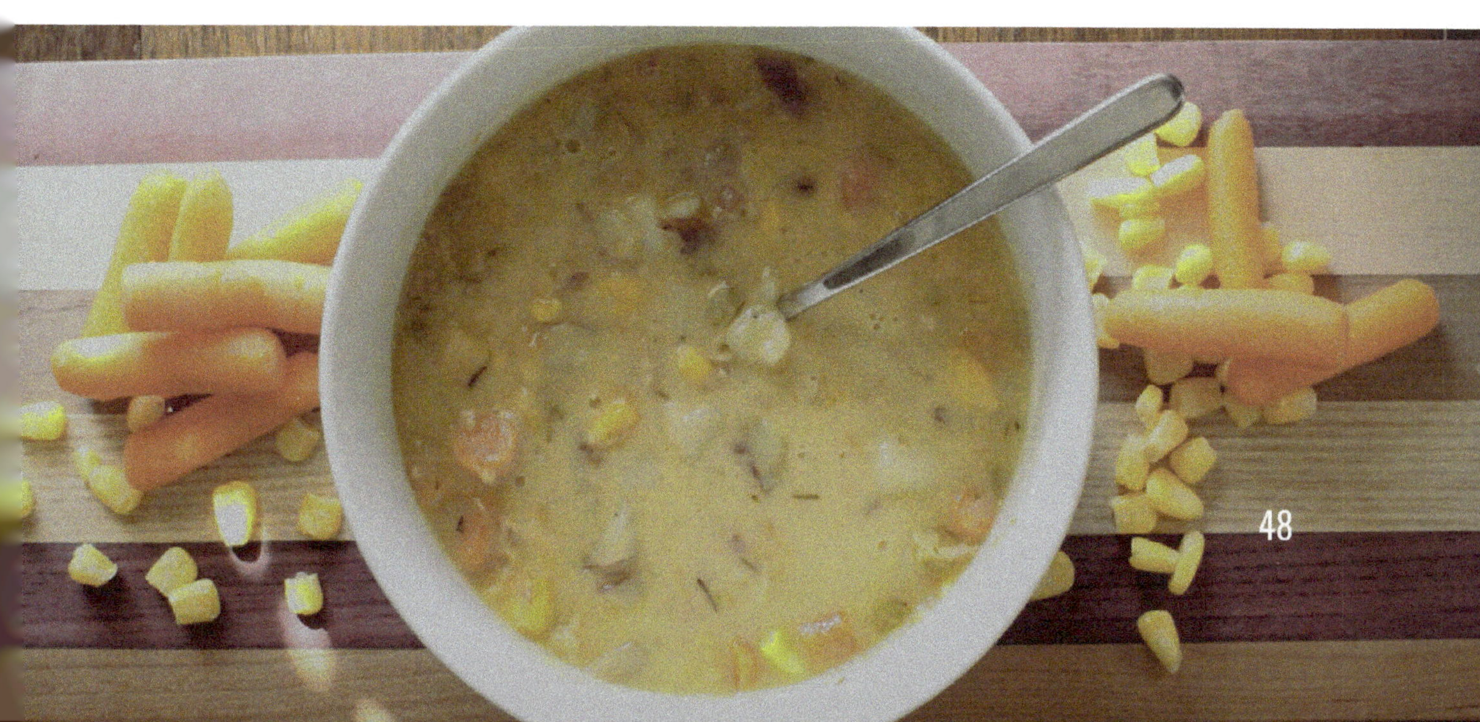

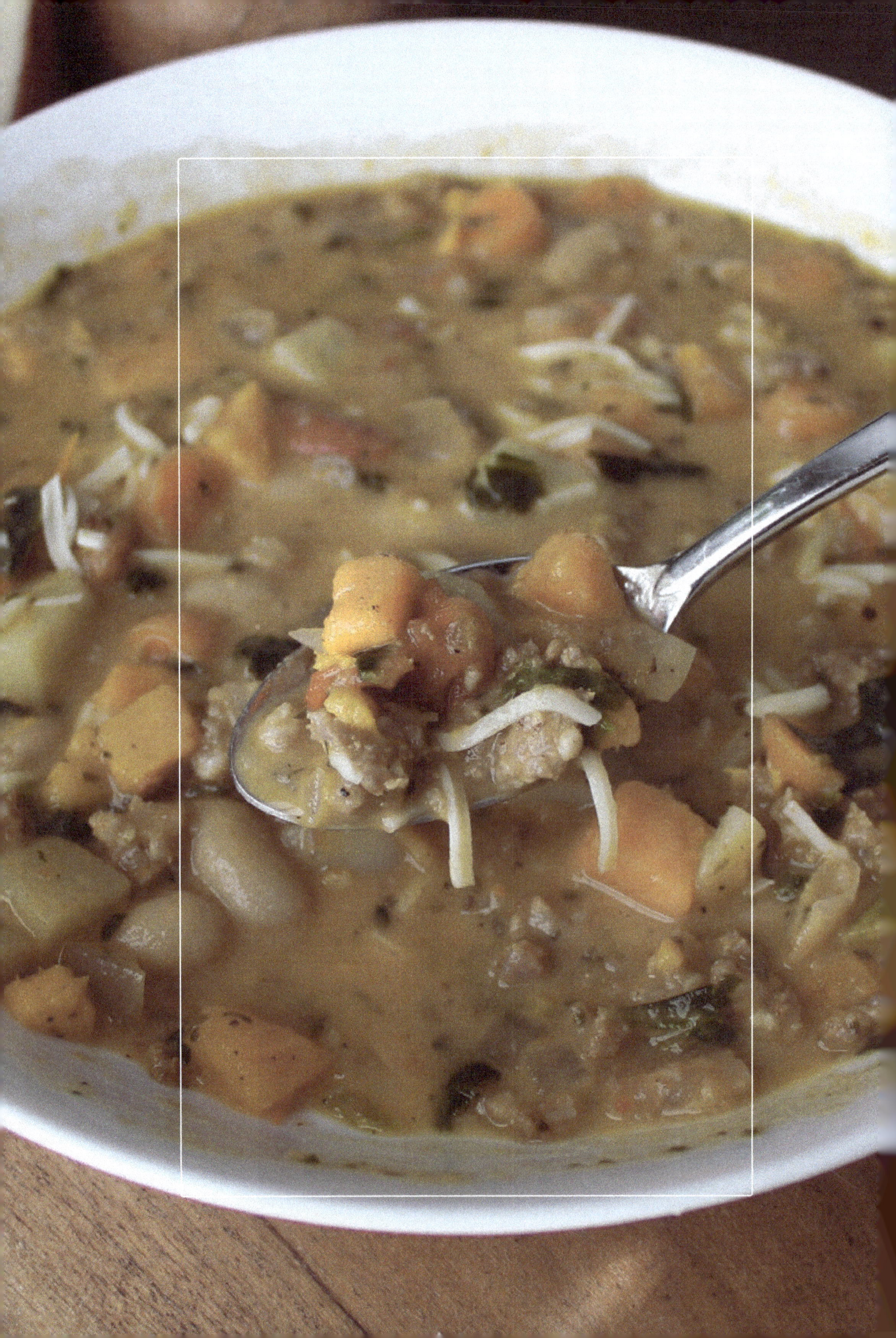

ITALIAN SAUSAGE + SWEET POTATO SOUP

YIELD: 6-8 SERVINGS PREP TIME: 10 MIN COOKING TIME: 35 MIN

Cozy, hearty, and spicy. This is the ultimate snow-day soup.

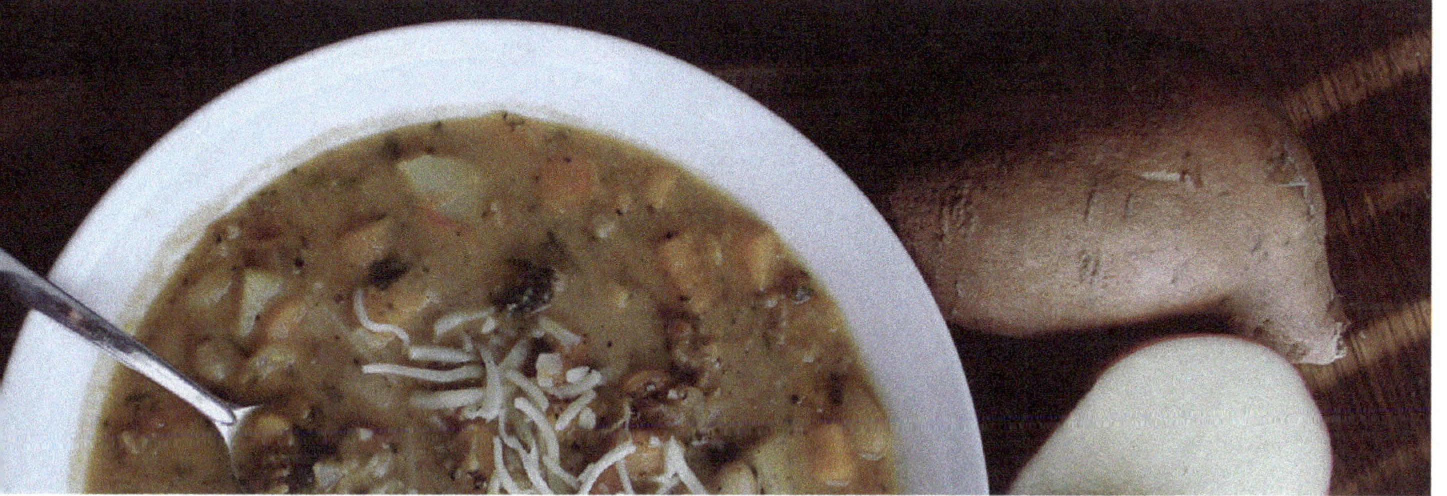

Ingredients

- 1 yellow onion
- 3 tbs minced garlic
- 2 sweet potatoes, peeled + diced
- 1 large red potato, washed and diced
- 1 lb ground hot Italian sausage
- 1 carton (32 oz) of vegetable stock
- 1 can of cannellini beans, rinsed
- 1 14 1/2 oz can petite diced tomatoes, drained
- 2 c frozen chopped spinach (or to taste)
- 1 c half and half or alternative
- salt, pepper, thyme, basil oregano

Directions

1. In a large stock pot over medium heat, add onion, garlic, and potatoes. Cook until onion is soft and fragrant.
2. Add in ground sausage and garlic, and season liberally with salt, pepper, thyme, basil and oregano.
3. When the sausage is just about done, add in the stock, beans, and diced tomatoes.
4. Bring to a steady simmer and cook until potatoes are fork tender.
5. Slowly stir in the half and half or your dairy-free alternative and return to a simmer for 10 minutes.
6. Add in the spinach last and simmer for 10 minutes more.
7. Serve with a sprinkle of cheese on top, or my favorite way- with a piece of provolone cheese at the bottom of your bowl and some toasted ciabatta bread.

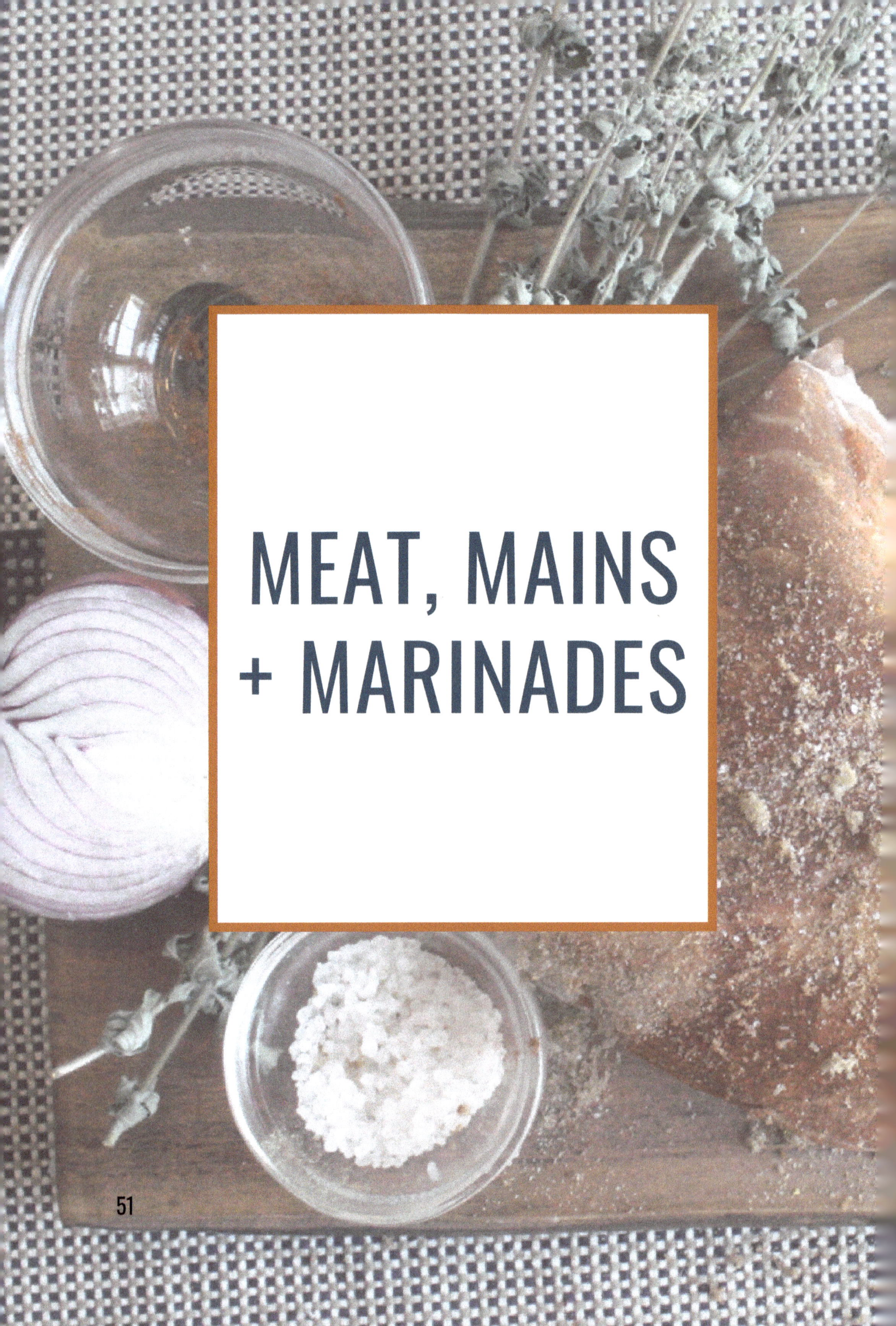

MEAT, MAINS + MARINADES

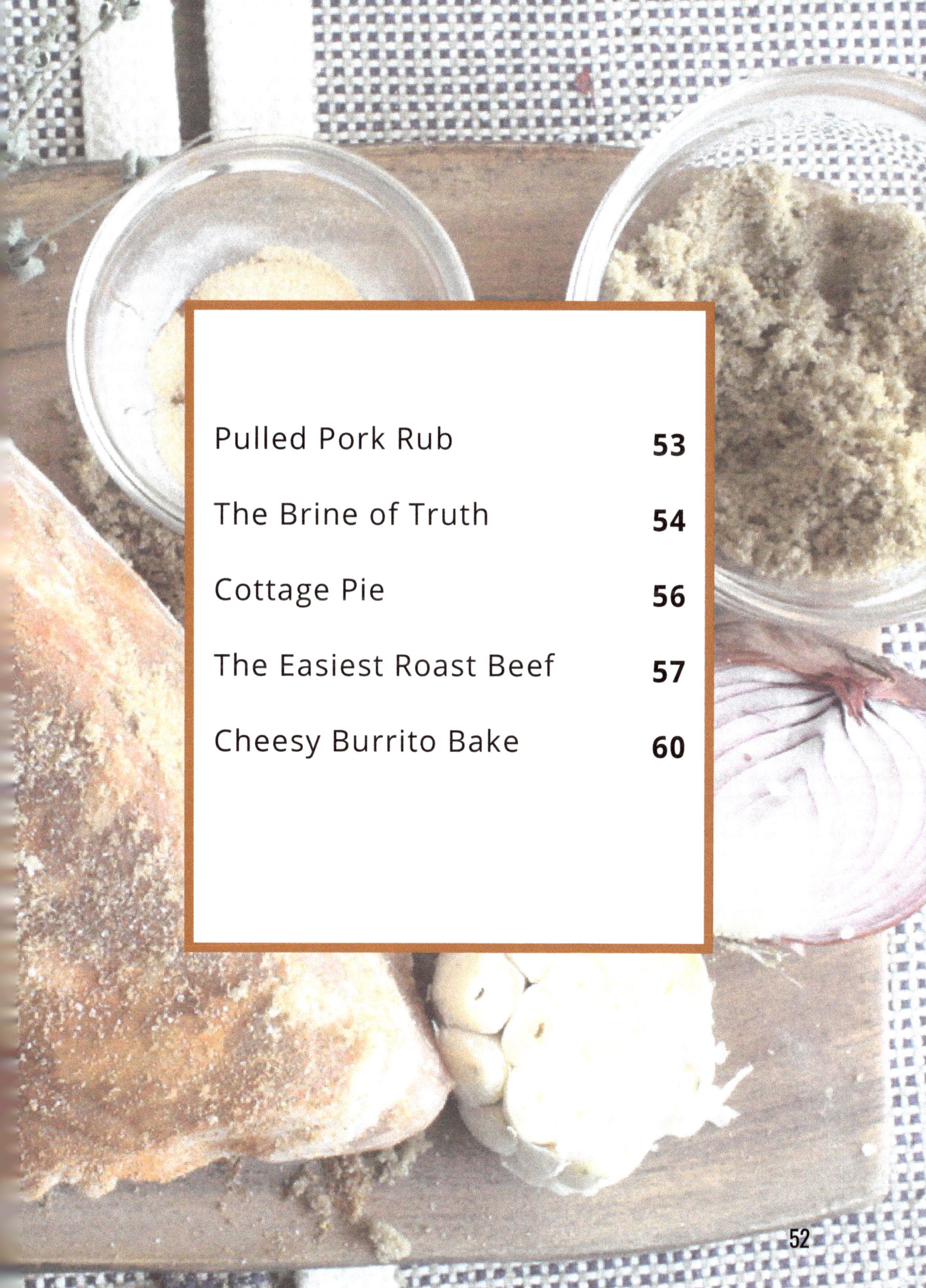

CLASSIC PULLED PORK RUB

YIELD: RUB FOR 1 ROAST   PREP TIME: 5 MIN   COOKING TIME: VARIES

A foolproof, simple rub for pulled pork. It's tasty and neutral so you'll be able to use the pulled pork with many recipes and cuisines without it overshadowing the flavor of your dish.

Ingredients

- 10 garlic cloves, peeled
- 1/2 c brown sugar
- 1 tbs salt
- 1 tbs black pepper
- 1 tbs onion powder
- 1 tbs garlic powder
- 1 tsp oregano
- 1 tsp paprika
- 1 tsp ground coffee
- 1 c beer or broth

Directions

1. Start by patting the meat dry with paper towels.
2. With scissors, trim off the excess fat. You'll want to leave a little bit to render down while it cooks.
3. Make ten 1-inch deep incisions all over the roast and insert a peeled clove of garlic into each one.
4. Mix the rest of the ingredients together in a small bowl.
5. Rub all sides of the roast with the spice mixture.
6. No need to sear! Toss it in the crock pot with 1 cup of beer or broth, until it falls apart easily, usually 4-6 hours on high (less if your crock pot runs hot like mine).
7. Once cooked, shred the pork for use in any recipe (like the Cuban Breakfast Burritos on p. 19).

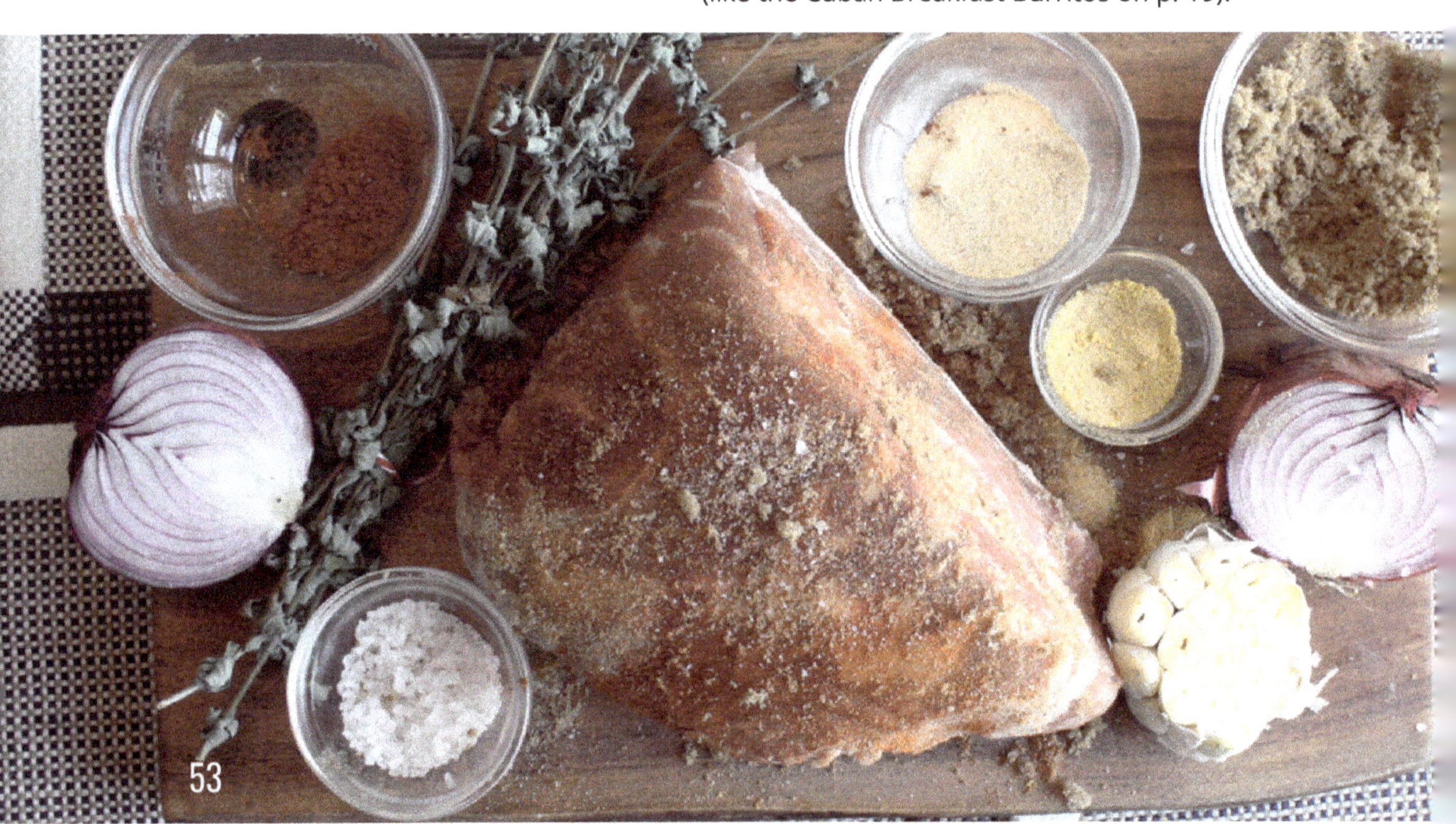

THE BRINE OF TRUTH

YIELD: 4 CUPS PREP TIME: 5 MIN BRINING TIME: 1-12 HRS

A brine born of desperation and a deep need for wings on a spring afternoon. Great for any poultry, whole or not! For large-scale brining, double or triple this recipe, and throw in some sliced lemons, oranges, and whole herb stalks throughout the brine process.

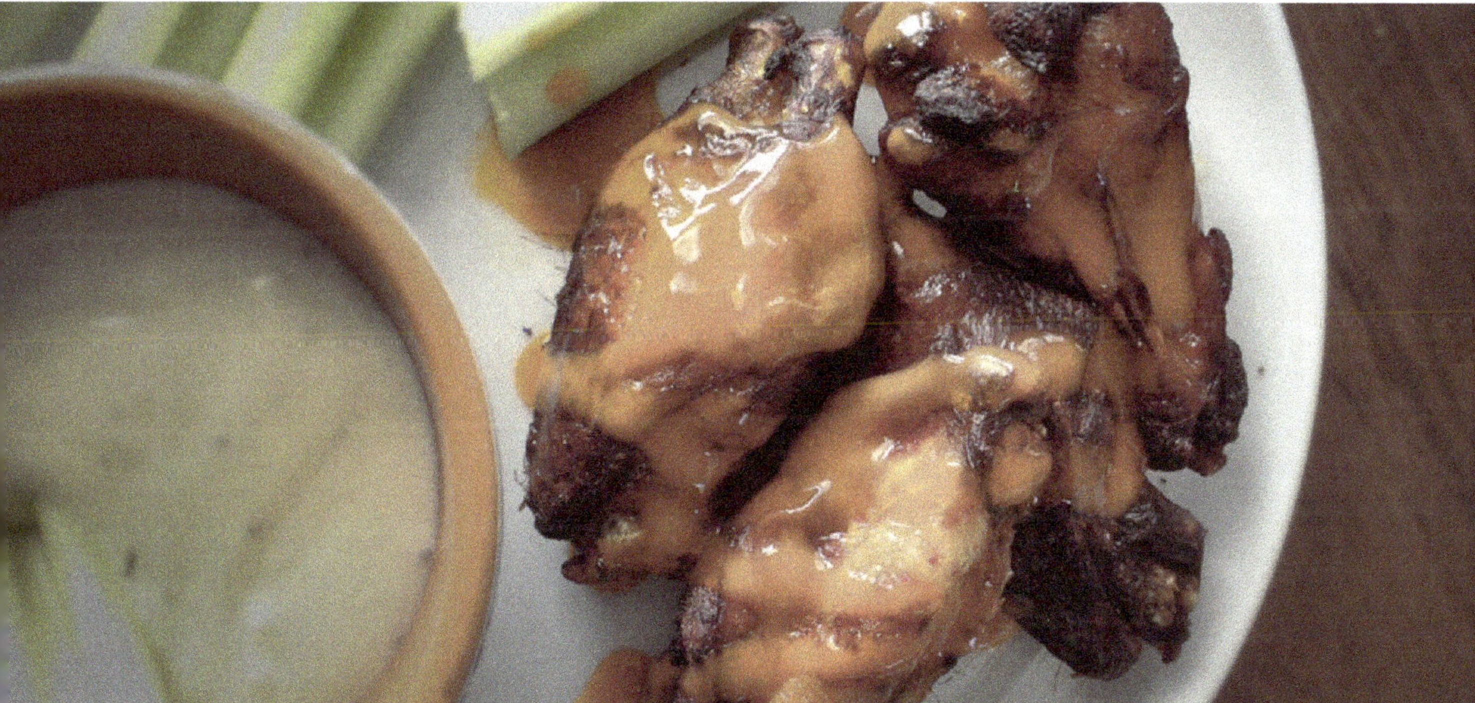

Ingredients

- 2 c water
- 2 c orange juice
- 2 bouillon cubes
- 1/2 c sugar
- 1/2 c salt
- 1/8 tsp nutmeg
- 1/8 tsp allspice
- 1/2 tsp cayenne
- 1 heaping tbs garlic
- 2 heaping tbs onion powder
- 1/3 c soy sauce

Directions

1. Combine all ingredients in a large pot over medium heat. Remove from heat when sugar and salt are completely dissolved, and before the solution comes to a boil. Let cool for 10 minutes.
2. Add in the poultry of choice- wings, thighs, etc. and cover.
3. Place in refrigerator for at least one hour but not more than 12.
4. Remove from brine, pat dry and use as usual for any recipe that calls for poultry.

one batch of this recipe is enough to brine up to 3 lbs of chicken!

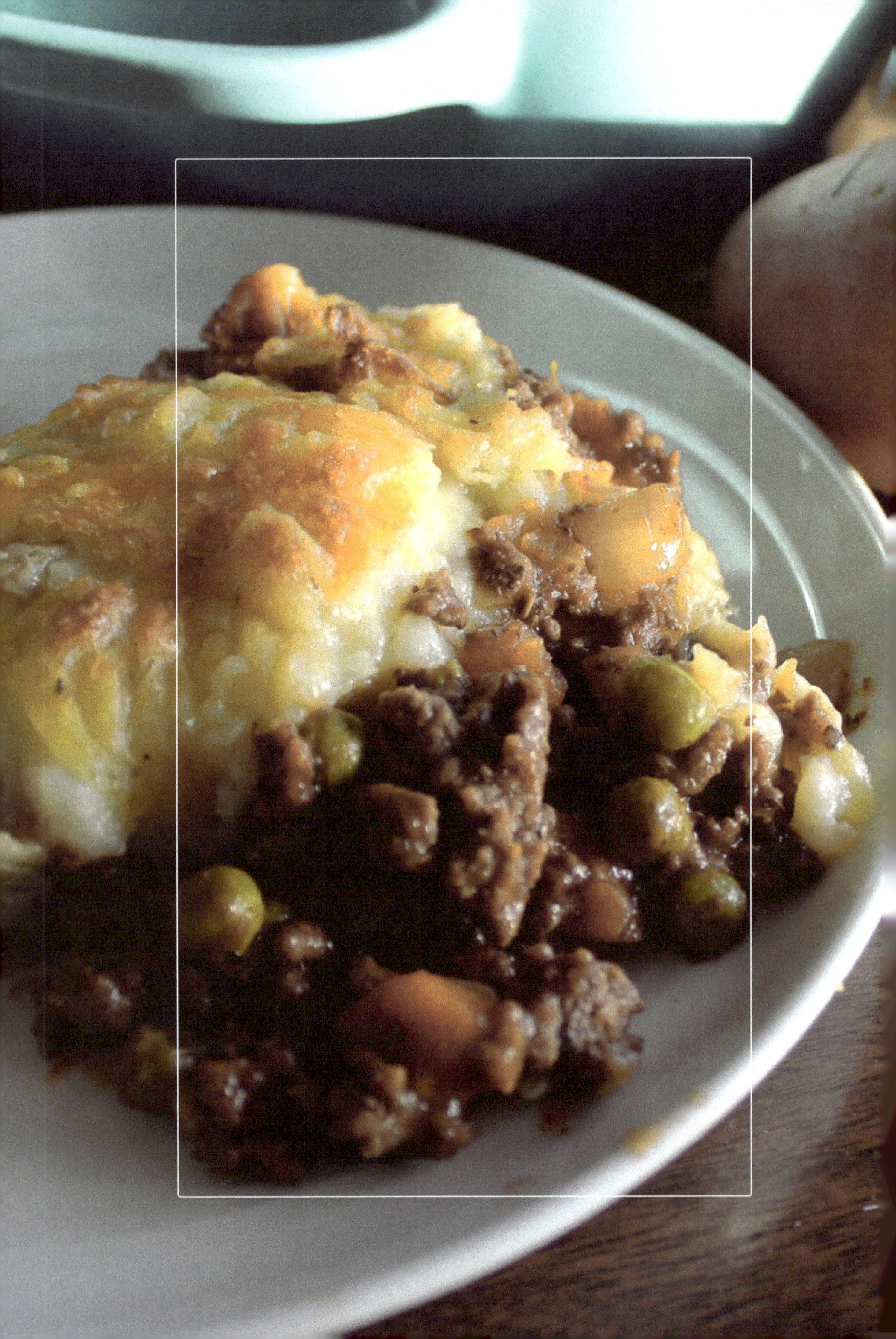

COTTAGE PIE

YIELD: 6-8 SERVINGS PREP TIME: 20 MIN COOKING TIME: 25 MIN

Fun Fact: not synonymous with shepherd's pie, which uses lamb instead of beef!

Ingredients

Mashed Topping

- 6-8 washed and diced potatoes
- 3/4 c cream or milk
- 3 tbs butter
- salt and pepper
- 1 c shredded cheddar
- 1/4 c sour cream

Filling

- 2 tbs oil
- 3 c frozen peas and carrots
- 3 cloves of garlic, minced
- 3 tbs tomato paste
- 1 lb ground beef
- 1 tbs flour
- 1 tbs thyme
- 1/2 tsp rosemary
- 1-2 tbs worcestershire sauce
- salt and pepper to taste
- 1 c red wine
- 1-2 c beef stock

use a variety of finely chopped mushrooms & vegetable stock in lieu of beef and beef stock, and plant-based alternatives for cheese, sour cream, butter and worcestershire to make it vegan friendly!

Directions

1. Preheat oven to 400 F.
2. Cover the potatoes in a pot with cold water and add a liberal amount of salt, bring to a boil for about 20 minutes.
3. While potatoes are cooking, add 1 tbs oil to a large skillet and begin cooking the beef. Add in the thyme, rosemary, salt and pepper while breaking the beef up into small bits, until the liquid is cooked off. Remove the beef from the skillet once cooked, and set aside.
4. Heat another tablespoon of oil in the same skillet. Saute the peas + carrots, onion, and garlic until soft, then add the beef back into the pan.
5. Sprinkle 1 tbs flour over the beef and veggies and mix in, letting it cook for a minute or two.
6. Pour in the worcestershire and red wine and let it cook down for 4-5 minutes.
7. Mix in the tomato paste thoroughly, and add in the beef stock. Let simmer until it has reduced to a beautiful thick gravy
8. While the skillet is simmering, and once potatoes are fork-tender, drain potatoes with a colander and mash well with the milk, butter, seasonings, sour cream and half of the cheese.
9. Place the ground beef mixture into the bottom of a 13x9 casserole dish in one even layer.
10. Dollop the mashed potatoes on top and gently spread out, and top with remaining cheese.
11. Bake at 400 F for 25-30 minutes or until toasted brown on top, and let sit for 15 minutes before serving.

EASIEST ROAST BEEF

YIEILD: 4-6 SERVINGS PREP TIME: 1 HR 10 MIN COOKING TIME: 45 MIN

Fancier cuts for parties and special occasions include prime rib, ribeye, or beef tenderloin. For a more budget friendly but equally flavorful option, choose a rump roast, sirloin tip, or bottom round roast. It's important to choose a cut that is gorgeously marbled with fat for maximum flavor. No strings, no searing... the hardest part is waiting to cut into it!

Ingredients

- 1 beef roast, 3-3 1/2 lbs
- garlic powder
- onion powder
- salt and pepper
- rosemary
- thyme
- olive oil

(oil from the garlic confit recipe would work deliciously here!)

Directions

1. Take the roast out of the refrigerator and packaging, generously salt all sides. Wrap with plastic wrap and let sit for 1-2 hours to bring it to room temperature.
2. Preheat oven to 375 F, with one rack placed in the center of the oven, and the other placed immediately beneath it.
3. Pat the roast dry with paper towels, and season liberally with salt, pepper, herbs, garlic and onion powder.
4. Drizzle with olive oil all over.
5. Place the roast directly on the center rack of the oven, with the fattiest side facing up, and place a baking sheet on the lower rack to catch the drippings. Roast at 375 F for 30 minutes.
6. After 30 minutes. lower the temperature to 225 F and continue to cook for another hour (in all, about 30 minutes per pound) or until internal temp reads 125-130 F for rare, 140-150 F for medium, or 150-165 F for well done.
7. When desired doneness is achieved, remove the roast from the oven and let it rest undisturbed for at least 20 minutes.
8. While the roast is resting, you can use the drippings from the baking sheet on the lower rack to make gravy if desired by adding the drippings to a small saucepan, bring to a simmer with 1 1/2 c of beef stock that has had 2 tbs flour completely mixed in with no lumps.
9. Whisk constantly and season as desired, until all lumps are gone and you have reached your desired thickness.
10. When you're ready, use a very sharp knife to cut into the roast, and enjoy!

this impressive yet simple roast is just as delicious (if not more delicious than) the deli sliced roast beef. you can use it for the beef crostini recipe on page 6! leftovers are great for steak sandwiches, salads, and more.

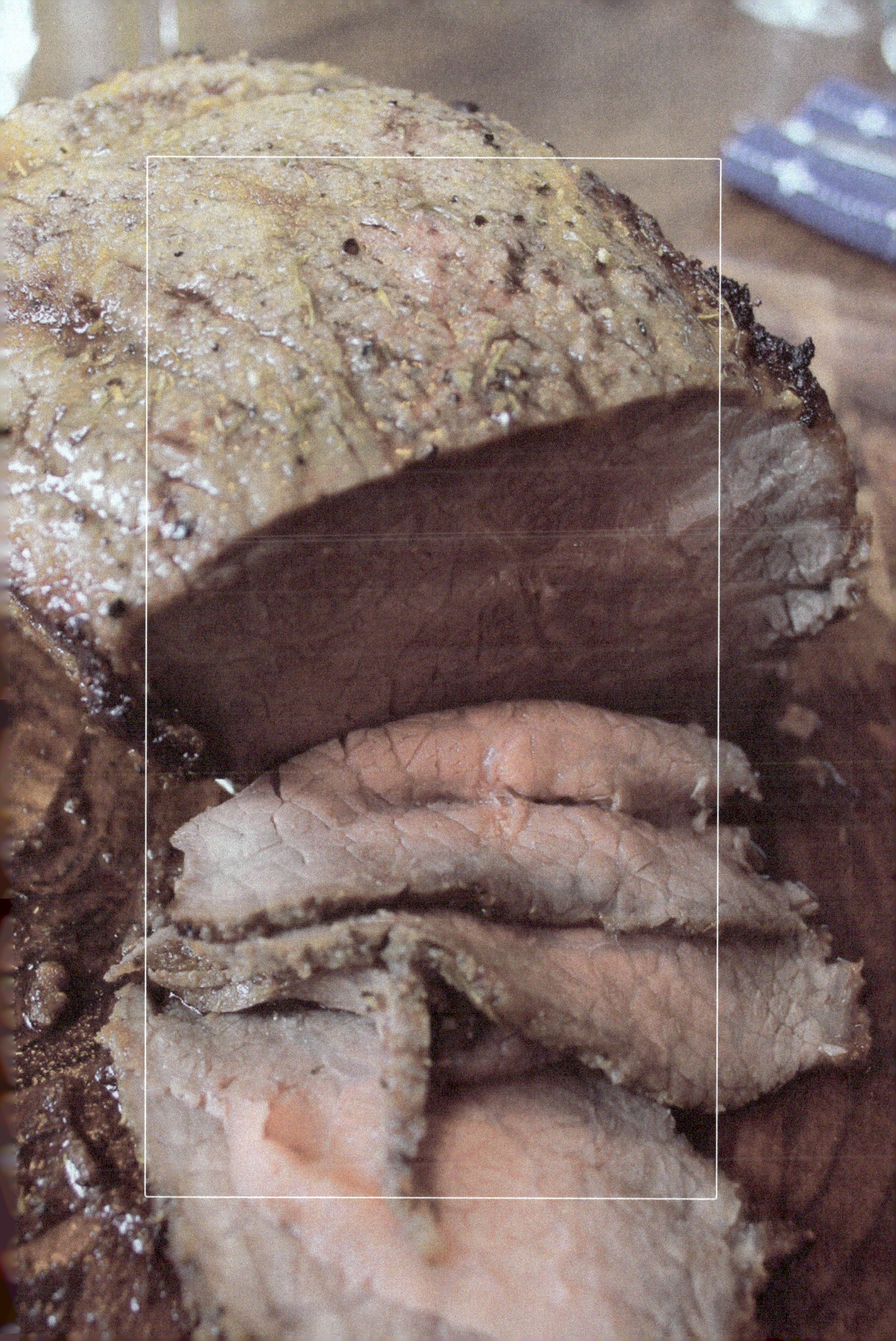

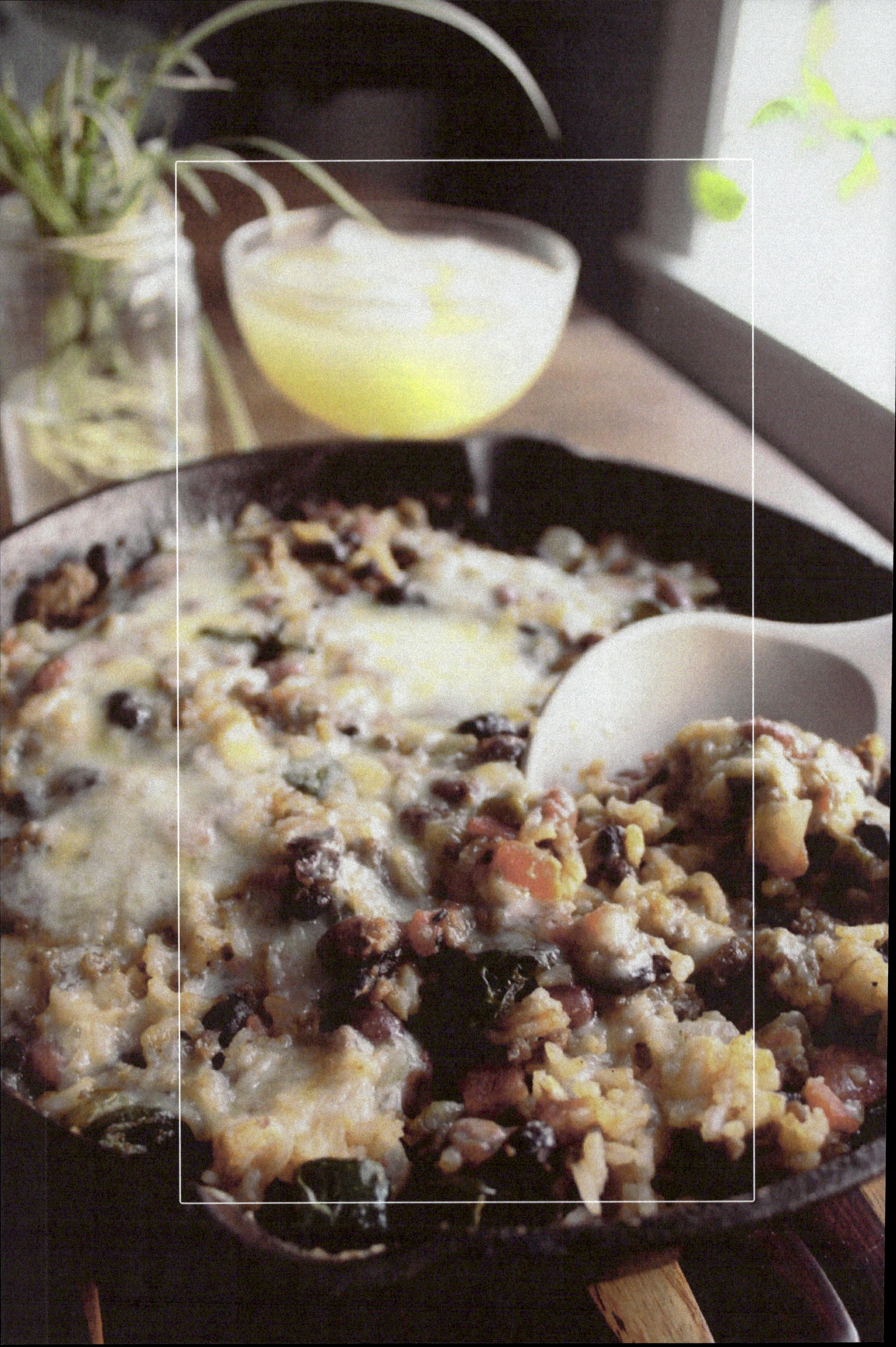

CHEESY BURRITO BAKE

YIELD: 4 SERVINGS PREP TIME: 25 MIN COOKING TIME: 20 MIN

Another recipe with endless opportunities for customization! Do you prefer less spicy food? Use a bell pepper! More spicy? Add a jalapeno or habanero. Not into rice? Try quinoa instead! Vegetarian? Omit the meat, add more beans, or use a meat alternative!

Ingredients

- 1/2 c white rice, washed
- 1/2 c chicken broth
- 1/2 c water
- 1 tbs tomato paste
- 1/2 onion, diced
- 1 large poblano pepper, diced
- 1 lb ground beef OR chopped/ground chicken
- 1 packet taco seasoning of your choice
- 1/2 can black beans, rinsed
- 1/2 can red beans, rinsed
- 4 oz can mild green chilies
- 10 oz can diced tomatoes
- 1/4 block of cream cheese
- 1 c shredded cheddar
- spices as needed, or in place of taco seasoning: salt, pepper, cumin, chili powder, paprika, oregano, garlic, onion

this is excellent as a meal on its own topped with sour cream or avocado, but also fabulous rolled up in a tortilla to eat on the go!

Directions

1. Cook rice: add rice, broth, water and tomato paste to a sauce pan or rice cooker. Mix to blend the tomato paste into the liquid. Turn rice cooker on, or if using the stovetop method, bring all to a boil, reduce heat to low and cover. Leave covered and undisturbed for 15-20 minutes.
2. While rice is cooking, cook the meat according to the instructions on the taco seasoning packet (if using). If not, saute the meat in a skillet over medium heat. Use about 1/2 tsp each of cumin, chili powder, paprika and oregano, and add the salt, pepper, garlic and onion powder to taste. From there, adjust to your liking!
3. When the meat is just about cooked through, add in the diced poblano and onion and cook until softened, about 4 minutes.
4. Rinse the beans, drain the chilies and tomatoes, and add to the skillet. Let simmer for 5 minutes.
5. Once some of the liquid has cooked off, mix in the cream cheese and half of the cheddar cheese til creamy and melty,
6. When the rice is done, gently fold it into the mixture in the skillet.
7. If using an oven safe skillet, top it off with the other half of cheddar cheese and broil on high for 2-3 minutes, until toasted and bubbly. If you don't have an oven-safe skillet, an 8x8 casserole will work just fine!

SWEETS

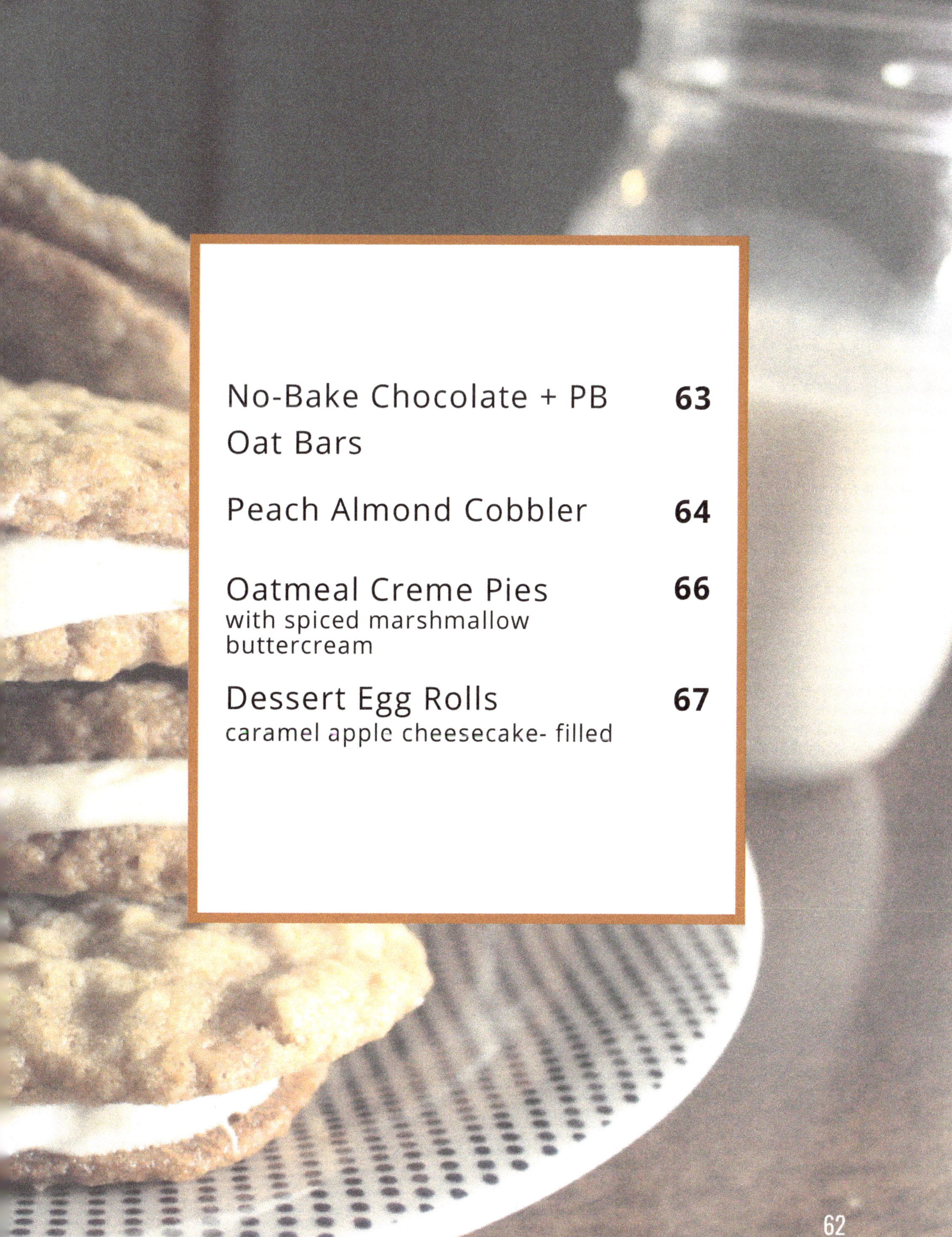

NO-BAKE CHOCOLATE + PB OAT BARS

YIELD: 9 SERVINGS PREP TIME: 15 MIN SETTING TIME: 30 MIN

Who has two thumbs and loves:
A. Chocolate, B. Not turning the oven on if I don't have to, and C. Dessert?

Ingredients

- 1 c semi sweet chocolate chips
- 1 c peanut butter
- 3/4 c butter
- 1/2 c packed brown sugar
- a pinch of salt
- 1 tsp vanilla extract
- 1 1/2 c quick oats
- 1 1/2 c coconut flakes (plus more for garnish)

Directions

1. Melt the butter in a sauce pan over medium-low heat, add in the brown sugar and stir constantly until smooth. Simmer gently for 3 minutes.
2. Remove from heat and mix in the vanilla and a pinch of salt.
3. Stir in the oats and coconut flakes to the brown sugar mixture and set aside.
4. In a microwave safe bowl, melt together the peanut butter and chocolate chips. It will take about three 45-second intervals at 50% power. Be careful not to overheat it or it will burn and be unsalvageable!
5. In the bottom of an 8x8 pan lined with parchment, pack down 3/4 of the oat mixture.
6. Spread 3/4 of the melted chocolate and peanut butter over the oat layer, and sprinkle the rest of the oat mixture on top of the chocolate.
7. Drizzle once more with remaining chocolate and top with a sprinkle of coconut flakes.
8. Refrigerate for 30 minutes or until set, then cut and serve.

** any leftovers should be stored in the fridge!

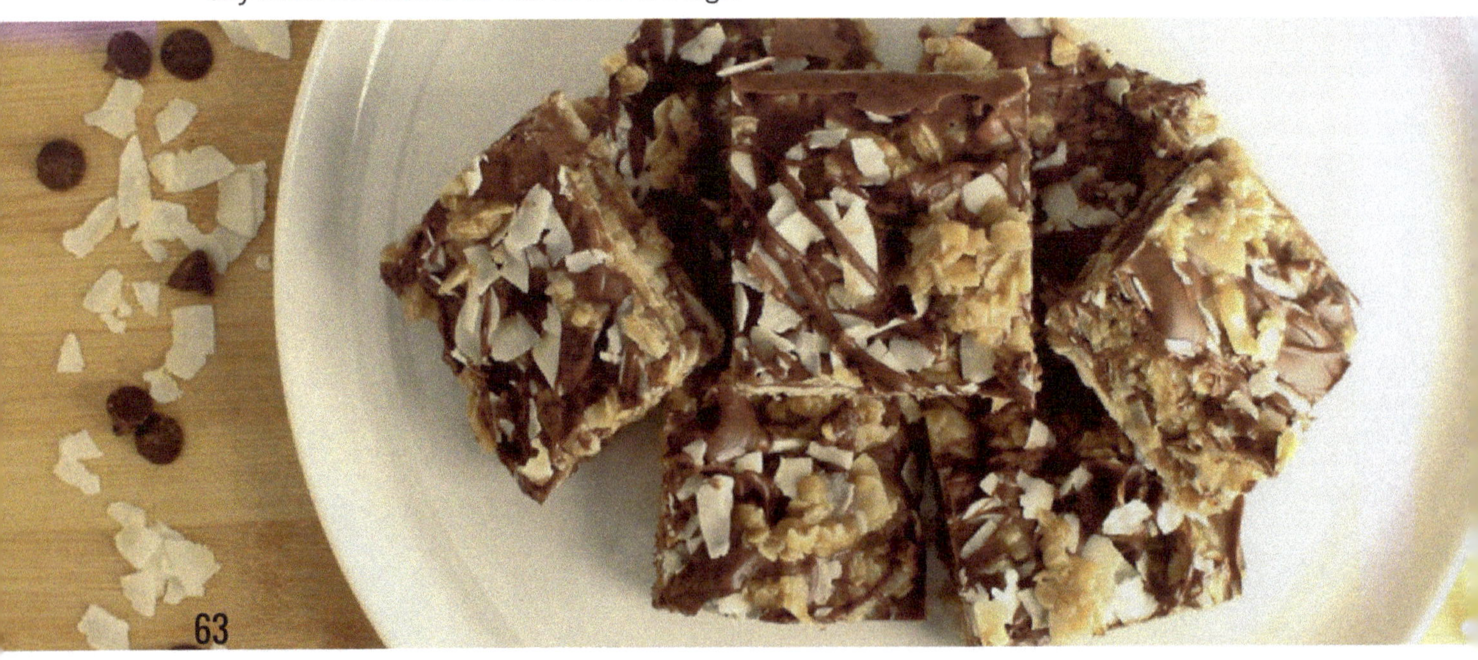

PEACH ALMOND COBBLER

YIELD: 6-8 SERVINGS　　PREP TIME: 10 MIN　　COOKING TIME: 1 HR

Easy enough to double for a crowd or whip up for an unexpected guest. You can substitute flour in this recipe for any 1:1 gluten free flour or use almond milk and vegan butter with results just as delicious and allergy friendly. Change it up with in-season fruit too!

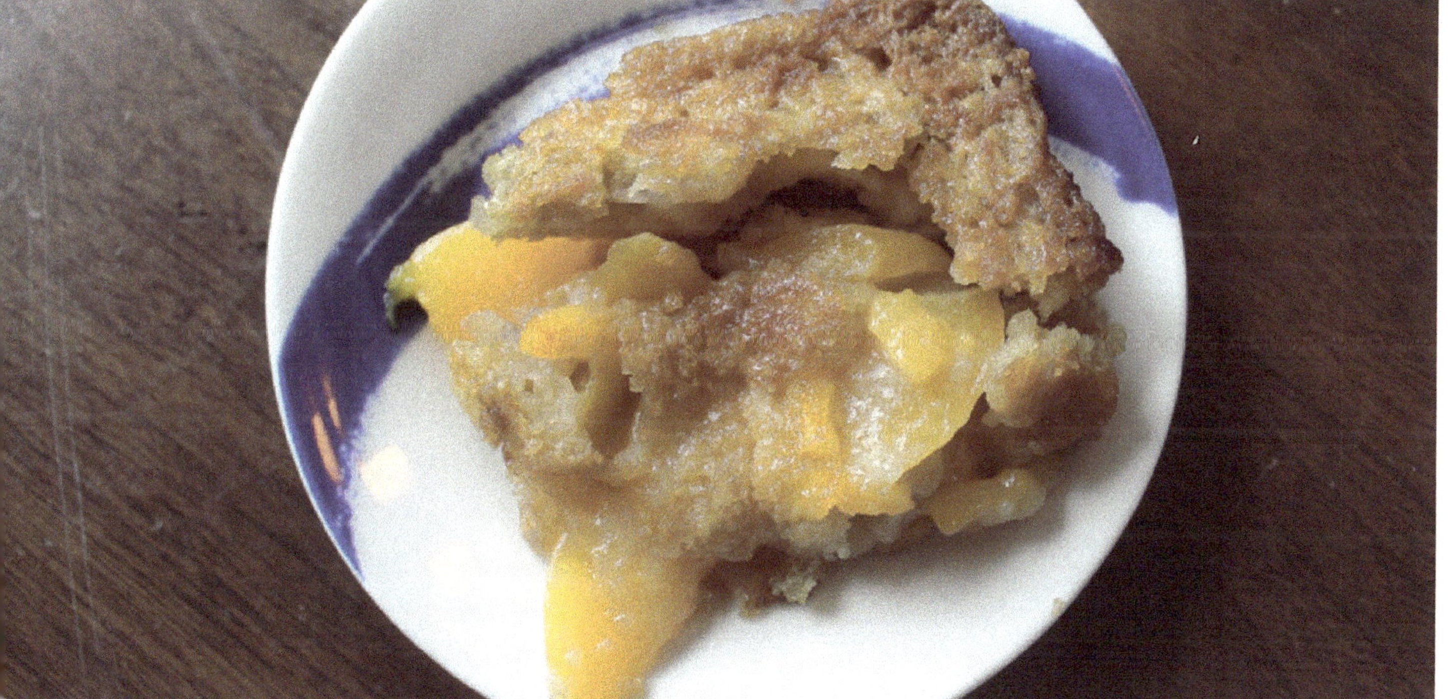

Ingredients

- 1 c butter, melted
- 1 c milk
- 1 c flour
- 1 c sugar
- 1 tbs baking powder
- 3 c fresh or frozen diced peaches
- 1 tsp almond extract
- 1 tsp vanilla extract

Directions

1. Heat oven to 350 F.
2. Pour melted butter into the bottom of a 9x9 baking pan.
3. In a separate bowl, mix together the milk, flour, sugar, baking powder, vanilla, and almond extracts until combined. Pour the batter into the baking dish right on top of the melted butter. Do not stir or mix it!!
4. Drop the fruit right on top of the batter, achieving a good cover over the batter.
5. Bake at 350 F for an hour, remove and serve warm with whipped cream or ice cream!

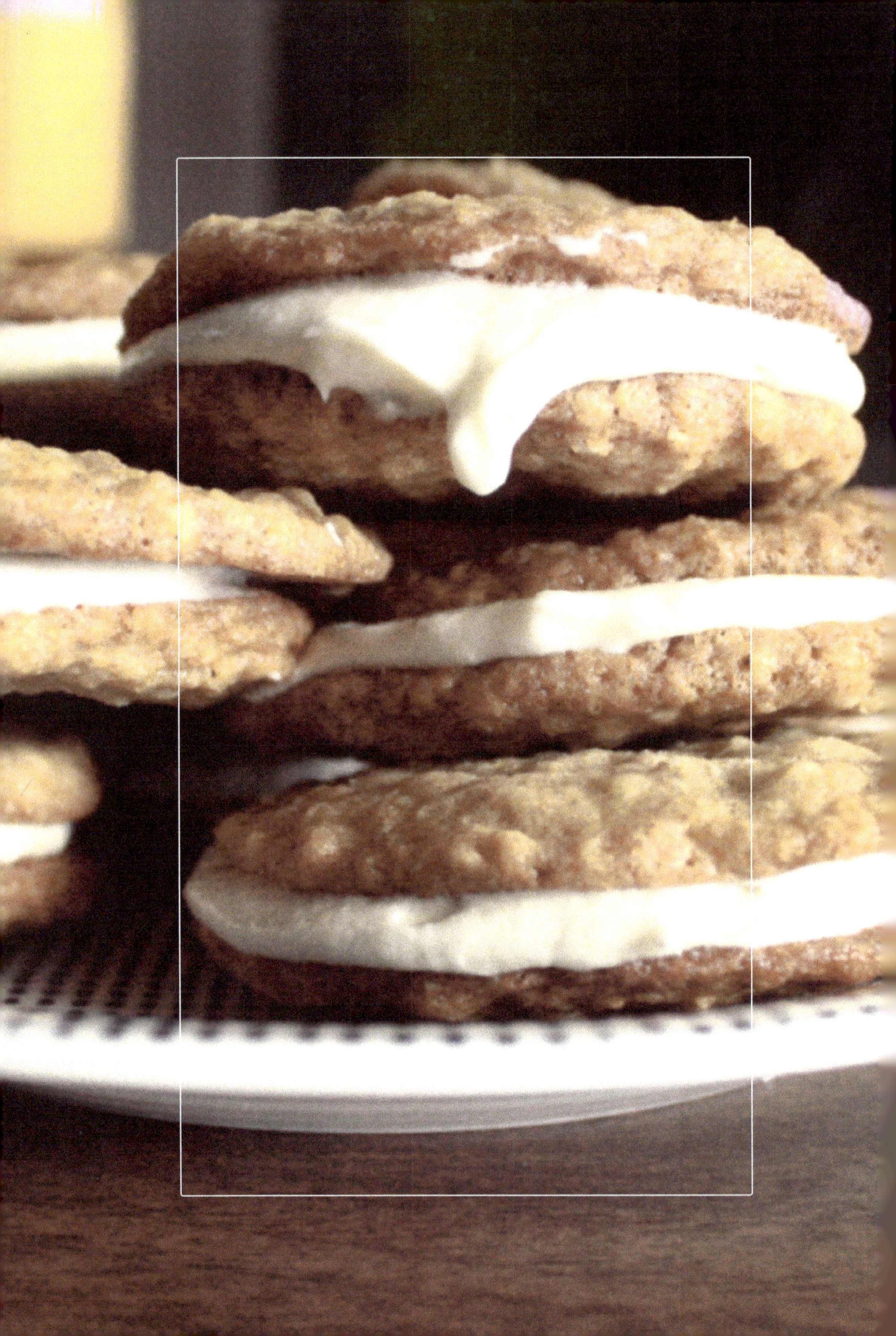

OATMEAL CREME PIES WITH SPICED MARSHMALLOW BUTTERCREAM

YIELD: 16 SANDWICHES PREP TIME: 20 MIN COOKING TIME: 10 MIN

Ingredients

- 2 sticks unsalted butter, softened
- 1 c granulated sugar
- 1/2 c packed dark browk sugar
- 1 egg
- 2 tsp vanilla extract
- 1 1/2 c flour
- 1 tsp cinnamon
- 1/8 tsp nutmeg
- 1 tsp baking soda
- 1/4 tsp salt
- 1/8 tsp baking power
- 1 1/2 c quick oats

Buttercream FIlling

- 1 stick unsalted butter, softened
- 2 cups marshmallows, melted (or use fluff)
- 1 tbs vanilla extract
- 1/4 tsp each: cinnamon, ginger and nutmeg
- 3 c powdered sugar, sifted
- 2 tsp whipping cream

Directions

1. Heat oven to 350 F.
2. With a hand mixer, cream together the butter and sugars until smooth, then beat in the egg and vanilla until combined and uniform in texture.
3. In a separate bowl, sift together the rest of the dry ingredients except for the oats.
4. On low speed, mix in the sifted flour until combined, then gently stir in the oats.
5. Shape the dough into 1 1/2" sized balls (about 2 tbs of cookie dough) and arrange with 2" space between each onto a parchment lined baking sheet.
6. Bake for 8-11 minutes or until golden brown around the edges. Let cool slightly before transferring to a wire rack to cool completely.
7. For the buttercream filling, use a hand mixer to combine butter and marshmallow/fluff with vanilla extract.
8. Sift together the spices and powdered sugar. Add half of the mixture to the butter and beat on low speed until combined. Repeat with the other half.
9. Add whipping cream 1 teaspoon at a time, whipping on high speed, until the buttercream is light and fluffy.
10. Using a spatula or piping bag, spread about 2 tbs of the buttercream on one cookie and top with a second. Repeat until you're out of cookies!
11. Best enjoyed after refrigerating overnight, but can also be served right away.

DESSERT EGG ROLLS

CARAMEL APPLE CHEESECAKE-FILLED

YIELD: 5 SERVINGS   PREP TIME: 10 MIN   COOKING TIME: 10 MIN

Ingredients

- egg roll wraps
- 1 apple, peeled, cored, and diced into 1/2 chunks (gala or cortland work well)
- 2 tsp cinnamon
- 1/4 tsp ginger
- 1/4 tsp nutmeg
- 1 tbs granulated sugar
- 2 tbs brown sugar
- 1/4 package (2 oz) cream cheese, softened
- water for sealing the edges
- oil for a semi-deep fry

caramel sauce

- 1 c granulated sugar
- 1/3 c water
- 3/4 c heavy cream
- 2 tbs butter
- 1 tsp vanilla extract

Directions

1. Make the caramel sauce first (or use store bought and skip to STEP 5): pour sugar into a sauce pan, gently shake to level it flat. Pour in the water, and turn the heat to medium. If you have a power-boil burner, keep it at medium-low.
2. Don't touch it! don't stir it, don't even think about it. Just keep an eye on it and wait for the sugar to completely dissolve. Once it looks clear, increase the heat a little bit and allow it to bubble steadily til it turns golden in color, like honey.
3. Remove from heat and stir in the heavy cream. It will probably foam and bubble or even spatter- this is normal.
4. Add the butter, stirring to melt it evenly throughout until it is smooth. Add vanilla extract and allow to cool to room temp before use.
5. In a small bowl, mix the diced apples with sugars and spices til well coated, and set aside.
6. Whisk together the softened cream cheese and 3 tbs of the caramel sauce (or to taste) until smooth.
7. In a small saucepan, heat about 2 inches of oil over medium heat.
8. Lay the egg roll wrap out like a diamond. Layer 1 1/2 tbs of the cream cheese mixture across the middle of the square. Top that with about 1 1/2 tbs of the apple mixture.
9. Wet all four edges of the wrap with water. Fold the corner closest to you up and over the apples to secure the filling beneath it. Fold the outer corners in to the center and press to seal any folds again.
10. Now roll the sealed bottom half up to the corner farthest from you. Use more water to seal corners if needed. Repeat steps 8-10 until you've used all the filling.
11. Gently place 2 rolls at a time into the hot oil, turning each one until browned all over.
12. Remove from oil, drain on paper towels and wait 5 minutes before serving. Dust with confectioner's sugar, use caramel sauce or any left over cream cheese filling for dipping.

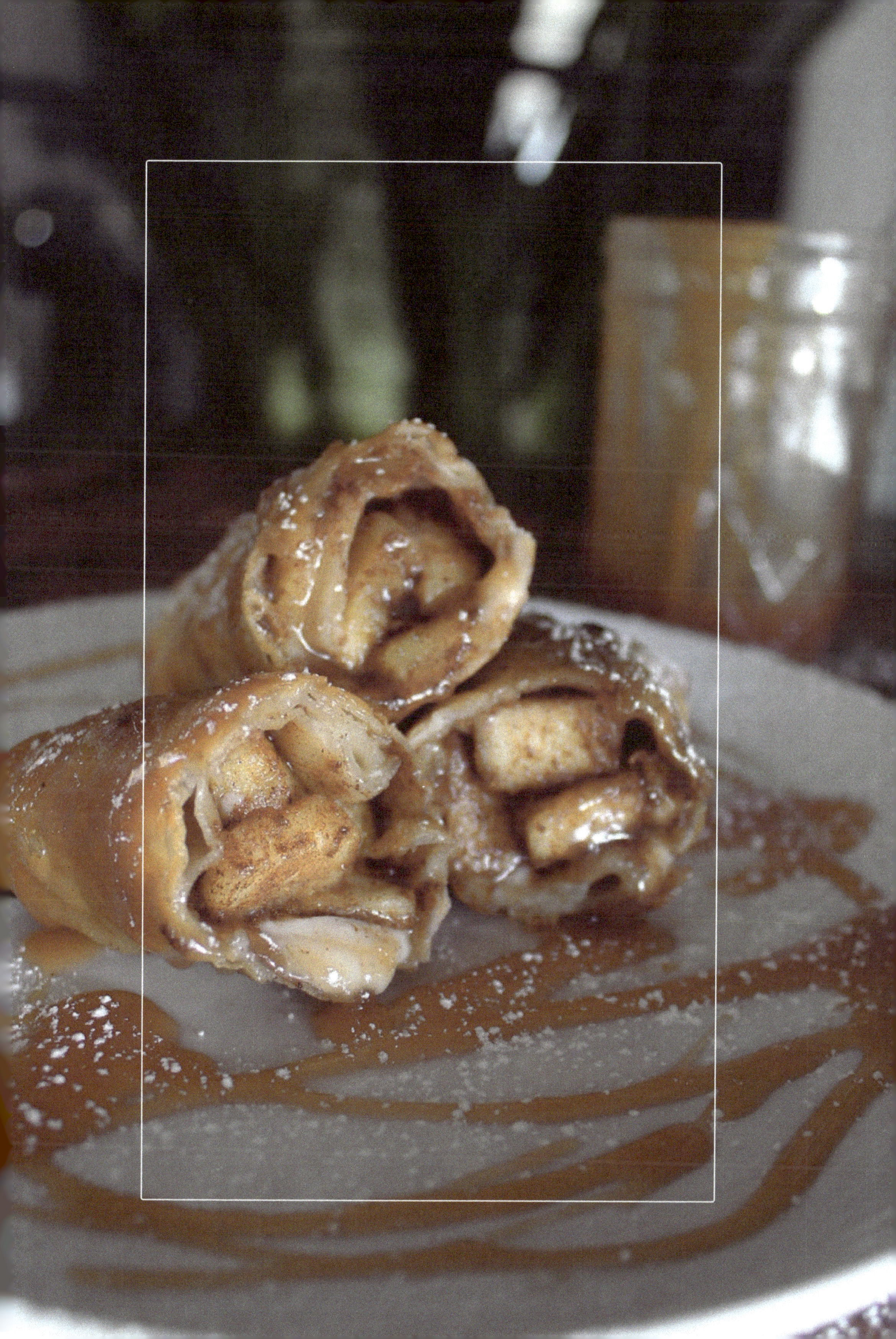

INDEX

DRY MEASURE CONVERSIONS

Cups	Tablespoons	Teaspoons	Ounces	Milliliters
1 c	16 tbs	48 tsp	8 oz	237 mL
3/4 c	12 tbs	36 tsp	6 oz	177 mL
2/3 c	10 + 2/3 tbs	32 tsp	5 oz	158 mL
1/2 c	8 tbs	24 tsp	4 oz	118 mL
1/3 c	5 + 1/3 tbs	16 tsp	3 oz	79 mL
1/4 c	4 tbs	12 tsp	2 oz	59 mL
1/8 c	2 tbs	6 tsp	1 oz	30 mL
1/16 c	1 tbs	3 tsp	½ oz	15 mL

FLUID MEASURE CONVERSIONS

Gallons	Quarts	Pints	Cups	Ounces	Liters
1 gal	4 qt	8 pints	16 c	128 oz	3.8 L
1/2 gal	2 qt	4 pints	8 c	64 oz	1.9 L
1/4 gal	1 qt	2 pints	4 c	32 oz	.95 L
	1/2 qt	1 pint	2 c	16 oz	480 mL
		1/2 pint	1 c	8 oz	240 mL
			1/2 c	4 oz	120 mL
			1/4 c	2 oz	60 mL
				1 oz	30 mL

MY KITCHEN NOTES

MY KITCHEN NOTES

MY KITCHEN NOTES

MY KITCHEN NOTES

MY KITCHEN NOTES

MY KITCHEN NOTES

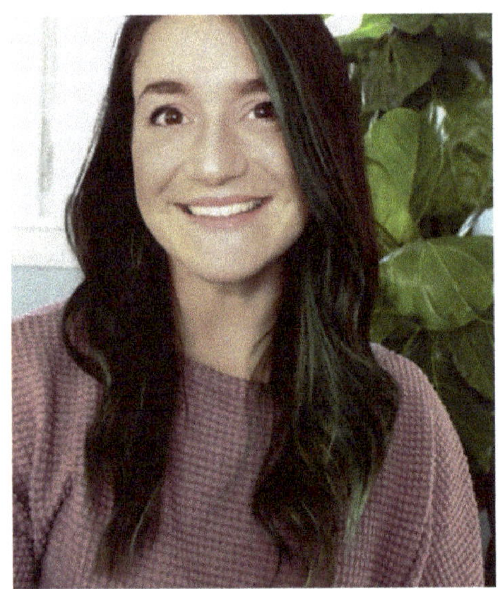

Abigail Martel is an elder emo millennial currently living in the lakes region of New Hampshire, USA. She lives with her husband Seth, her Treeing Walker hound Darla, her mini Dachshund William, and tabby cat named Meow Meow. When she is not cooking, she enjoys at least 40 hobbies, including gardening, tie dyeing, collecting house plants, painting, traveling, outdoor activities, and power sports. She hopes to someday open and operate a food truck, cannabis bakery, or restaurant!

Her first cookbook, Tried and True: Recipes from My Family to Yours, was published in 2016 and is available on lulu.com.

www.ingramcontent.com/pod-product-compliance
Lightning Source LLC
LaVergne TN
LVHW070533110826
845147LV00017BA/980

* 9 7 9 8 2 1 8 1 0 5 3 7 2 *